Wint

For all those who shared the Bookshop days, and for the wonderful young people now who are struggling for a better world

Winter at the Bookshop

Sylvia Riley

Sheila

Happy Birthday
love from Sylvia
xx

Five Leaves Publications

Winter at the Bookshop
Sylvia Riley

Published in 2019 by Five Leaves Publications
14a Long Row, Nottingham NG1 2DH
www.fiveleaves.co.uk
www.fiveleavesbookshop. co.uk

ISBN: 978-1-910170-66-3

Printed in Great Britain

Contents

Trotsky's Other Son

'Trotsky's Other Son' was chosen by Karl Miller of the London Review of Books *for the* New Stories 8 *Arts Council Anthology. Years later it was found in a second-hand bookshop in Australia by Bob Gould of Ozleft, who recognised Pat Jordan, although the names were changed, and he put the story on the web.*

Some years ago I lived in that part of the city which is known as St Ann's. Back then it was a sprawling area of industrial and pre-industrial houses set in cobbled hilly streets, to the north of the city centre. You walked along Parliament Street and turned down by the Milton's Head, passing Victoria Station and into a dirty old railway tunnel. Dim light from the constantly-lit lamps shuddered around the tarred wooden walls and pools of rainwater on the mud floor. The smell of sulphur came strong and overhead was an arc of black nothingness shared with unseen rattling trains. The tunnel was dark and so long that when you walked down it you forgot about daylight, and it always came as a shock at the other end.

Leaving the tunnel, you stepped out blinking into St Ann's. Across the road, standing guard at the edge of the area like a grey fortress with its barred blank-faced windows, was a Victorian disease hospital, by this time devoted solely to treating venereal disease. Past the mass of the hospital the streets sloped down into Union Road, wide and dirty and noisy. House doors stood open, children and dogs and old people spilled from them on to the pavements. Branches of privet and ancient lilac trees pushed their way up between slate roofs and outside lavatories. Willowherb lodged where it could. The pavements, which were of many kinds of brick, were stained with dust, spilt ice-cream, dog turds, rotting fruit, lolly sticks, bits of disintegrating cardigan and other matter which had irreparably lost its form and could only be guessed. Factories and churches and cream-painted pubs were pushed in between houses. In spite of traffic, packs of fat pigeons roamed about near the kerb edge and in the gutters, picking up spilt food outside the chip shops. They even crossed the road by foot. Somewhere there was an ancient well dedicated to St Ann. Nobody seemed to know where it was. It had probably been built over in those days in the last century when, next to Calcutta, Nottingham had the worst slums in the British Empire. The oldest and dirtiest buses ran the circumference of the area. Teachers at the schools drove into St Ann's in the mornings and straight out again at four o'clock, leaving it untouched.

Turning by the Oliver Cromwell pub and into the main thoroughfare of Great Alfred Street, you saw a renaissance-style Methodist chapel, with pillars and portico and a wide sweep of steps, which was now a rubber-tubing factory. On the opposite side was a second-hand bookshop. In its window an assortment of tatty paperback books was laid out in lines, and highly-coloured American comics and packets of nylons and crayons were strung across the back of the window on a piece of string. A few dead flies lay scattered over the books, and a black cat was blissfully asleep in the sunshine which managed to penetrate through the dusty window. Here, like a yucca moth giving and taking from its plant, lived Pat Jordan.

Pat was small, thickset and muscly, with large shovelly hands near his body, like a mole's, and he seemed to have a disproportionately large head, as a baby's is to its body. He was nearly totally bald, and perhaps because of it his age was hard to place. He seemed old and yet unborn, there was something very foetal about him. He wore plastic tortoiseshell spectacles which had broken at the bridge, and he stuck them together by holding them over a gas-flame until the plastic melted. As they kept on snapping and he kept on sticking them in this way he wore a progressively more owlish expression as his eyes seemed to get closer and closer together. From the front of the shop he sold second-hand books and comics, and in the back room he kept his duplicator ever turning, churning out documents and political statements and a weekly news-sheet. On the shelves around the walls were pamphlets, mostly by Lenin and Trotsky. The shop front was always pushing with children, and when he was working in the back room Pat operated a type of rigid prefect system worthy of the board schools. Any child caught thieving would expect — and get — very rough justice, St Ann's justice, from the boy in charge. There was great brutality in those days and in that place, and Pat was part of it. Hating still came completely naturally to him, he was not caught up with any ideas of social service or condescension.

Over the shop was the rest of the house, smelling of damp and cats. The stairs wound round twice, jutting into the rooms with the curves in their journey. The rooms were tiny, almost like large cupboards. There is something about tiny rooms that I like. They can be stultifying and smells linger in their brickwork, but you can expand your being and almost feel it hit against the walls, as though they are containing it, holding it while you grow. This can become intolerable, but it's better than wobbling disembodied in a vast room, or having all the objects in a well-planned room conspire against you.

Pat's room contained a low single bed heaped high with old blankets and about three old eiderdowns that different people had given him so he wouldn't be cold. Filthy curtains hung at the window, which was lodged permanently closed by a huge spanner which served instead of the missing catch. The wallpaper in here, as in the rest of the place, was dusty and old and looked like the kind of pattern which fluttered from bombsites. Around three sides of the room were piles and piles of documents and old chewed newspapers and correspondence. The floor was littered with books and boxes of staples and rusting staples that had spilled from the boxes. Mould attacked clumps of shoes. In a corner was a heap of dirty shirts which he periodically kicked aside in order to play on the lidless gramophone underneath his one record — 'Under Moscow Skies' — sung very slowly in French. The catch on the door didn't work, and so it was liable to bang all night if it was windy — the place was full of draughts and if the wind blew outside it blew inside too — keeping the occupants of the house awake.

I had left home to fly-post and demonstrate during the Cuban Missile Crisis, and never went back. When you have spent several days thinking the world is about to be blown up things are never the same afterwards. There were many of us for whom that was true, and many who did go home again afterwards were effectively riven from their families in spirit.

Pat could be very stern. 'You must study,' he would say. He pulled out a table from the heaps of mouldering documents and rubbish in his cellar, and set it up in my room for me to work on. 'The working class needs its people to know as much as they can. You owe it to your class as well as yourself to develop.'

* * *

For breakfast we all ate ice-cream from a van, even in the winter. Breakfasting from a tub of splintery ice with lashings of butterscotch was much better than being at boring old home eating boring old cereal before rushing off to boring old work. I was permanently afflicted with the adolescent curse of boredom. Pat boiled a kettle for tea practically non-stop throughout the day, and conducted fiendish sessions of mass egg-boiling, enough to last several days at once, to save himself the bother of cooking. We ate pork chops with baked beans or lamb chops with peas — the lamb he casseroled in the oven by placing it in the frying-pan and balancing a rusty old cake tin over the top. I liked to watch him cook. It seemed as though it was just part of his function as a magician — a touch here, and there was a meal, a touch there, and there was an up-to-the-minute news-sheet and a room full of people waiting to staple it together and put it into envelopes.

He would suddenly take off for whole weeks with a moment's notice. 'Well I'm off now, if the bailiffs come round tell them the duplicator isn't mine...' The first time I heard this I was scared stiff, but I soon got used to it. His attitude to money was a mixture of disregard as to where it came from and indifference as to where it went. He took not the slightest notice of any bill until the final demand came. The gas bill would come. He would empty the gas-meter, find there wasn't enough money inside because he had paid the electricity bill with most of it, and so he would open up the coinbox on the telephone. Those bills and any connected with the working of the duplicator were the only ones he paid fully. Other people were sent odd pounds whenever they complained.

'But that bill's for nine pounds!' I cried, the first time I saw him put a pound note in an envelope.

He waved a hand dismissively, as though he was the creditor. 'Doesn't matter. This will keep them quiet.'

* * *

Pat's first talk to us was on the relevance of Marxism to everyday life, and he used the simple example of the straw that broke the camel's back, to give us the idea of the difference between a qualitative change and a quantitative change. We were very young, and it was like being back at a kind of delightful school, with simple learning but no teachers. As Marxists, he said (with some exaggeration) we must recognise that everything, all matter, moved always, that nothing stood still, and that attitudes based on the forcing of stasis or 'standards' or 'order' were both evil and — probably more importantly — futile. We must recognise that matter moved and changed and became transmuted, learn to build upon that knowledge, and never attempt to deny or thwart the movement or push of life. In a sense, he said, the parable of the shifting sands is incomplete: you have to build upon shifting sand because that is the only kind there is. Instead of being inauthentic adults whose only task in life was to carry out what our employers commanded, we suddenly became children again with invisible building bricks, getting the feel of impermanence, learning to create, destroy, create. My vocabulary book, abandoned when I left school, was pulled out of my old satchel, and it suddenly burst with a crop of new words — helot, hegemony, latifundist, stakhanovite, putsch — words that thrilled me and that I wouldn't have learned from any other source.

Pat's attitude to the children who came into the shop varied according to his mood. They regarded him with awe-touched suspicion, relieved by bursts of sudden, completely unprovoked enthusiasm. He was authoritarian, but mad. He was liable to punch the boys and use extreme convoluted obscenities to them. He was merely extremely rude to the girls. This never made him unpopular. Many children whose parents were at work until five or six o'clock came straight to the bookshop from school, particularly in the winter, and Pat never turned them out even if they didn't buy anything. He told big lies about everything and everybody, and this seemed to appeal to the children. 'Here, are you really old Pat's stepmother?' I was asked by Alec, who helped in the shop. My mouth fell open, while the other children called and whistled and jostled by the paraffin heater. Pat often told them stories. One story which started its life in the back rooms had found its way, via Romolo, another of the boys who worked for Pat, into the shop. 'Be quiet, you lot,' he hollered, 'and when he comes back Pat'll tell you all about Trotsky's son.'

One of the pamphlets in the back room had been dedicated by Trotsky to his elder son — *Leon Sedov, Son, Fighter, Friend* — commemorated in epithets of granite. He had been murdered by Stalinists as he lay in a Paris hospital. This was very sad, but I was a nasty little thing and chock-full of spite and I didn't like having my heart wrung. I preferred Trotsky's other son. I've never subsequently heard of him outside of Pat's conversation, and I have no idea if he really existed. Pat claimed to have read a book about him, and so was constantly able to come out with nuggets of fresh information. When, in what was in our understanding, Marxism became too much for me, I would insist, 'Tell us about Trotsky's *other* son.'

According to Pat, Trotsky's other son wasn't political at all. The atmosphere in his home had been thick with politics since he was born, and it merely bored him. He ran off to join a circus. 'Let's see, what was his name…' Pat snapped his fingers trying to recall it. He told of the acrobats and the clowns, of Spangles the bareback rider who was in love with Trotsky's son ('Spangles?' mouthed the more sophisticated backroom contingent. 'Well you know what I mean. In translation,' was the impatient reply). But Trotsky's son didn't care about anybody except

Mitsi, the pretty dappled horse who danced and curtseyed. He saved titbits for her, and when she led the other horses out into the ring his heart almost burst with excitement as she nodded her head to one of the clowns and danced in time to the music while people cheered. Pat told of Trotsky's son's life from day to day, the hardships due to the famine and, as the revolution degenerated, persecution by the authorities. Finally the circus was rounded up and sent to the salt mines, accused of misleading the masses. The conjurer was accused of 'deceiving the people'; the clowns of 'performing acts lacking in socialist content'. Then one time, whether due to a fit of pique or moral earnestness I don't know (probably the latter), Pat over-reached himself and etched in a deathbed conversion to Trotskyism in Siberia. I never really believed in him after this.

Pat escaped from St Ann's just before the sociologists descended, when treatises and theses were written, statistics compiled and analyses made of them. American photographers came with astronomically expensive cameras to photograph rats and rubbish. Shamed, the council made immediate plans to pull down the area, to literally wipe it from the face of the earth. New concrete blocks appeared, the old pattern of the streets and their Cromwellian names were wiped out, and across the acres of rubble over Hutchinson Street many small fires crackled and smoked, like hellfire trying to break out. No longer walled up in his bookshop, Pat moves around — London, Brussels, Addis Ababa, Paris…

St Ann's is a long way behind him now. Most of us proved Pat's dismal expectations correct as to our revolutionary worthiness. We all reneged in one way or another, either from convenience or simple laziness. I haven't seen any of the comrades for years. But the other day on the bus I bumped into Alec, Pat's paper-boy. He is grown up now and married and working at Gedling Colliery. He asked if I'd heard anything of old Pat. I shook my head. Then he turned and said with enthusiasm, 'Here, do you remember Trotsky's son and Spangles and the horse? I was telling my missis about that when we were courting. What happened to them in the end?'

Winter at the Bookshop

Written to celebrate the birthday of Pat Jordan, born 17th July 1928, the son of Marie-Louise and John Jordan.

Winter at the Bookshop was a raw, warm, cold experience. Raw with chapped fingers clinging to kettles of boiling water from the gas-stove, multiple draughts whistling up and down the stairs; warm and sparkling with friendship, tiny coal-fires and everlasting hopeful activity. We went about heavy with knitted jumpers and perpetually booted, clutching hot water bottles and swathed in blankets when sitting in armchairs in the kitchen. As soon as he saw Pat laying the pieces of coal and firelighters, Tom the Bookshop cat would go into a swoon of ecstasy.

'This is human magic, Tom,' explained Pat. Once the fire got going and started spilling its ash into the hearth, Tom curled himself round and went to sleep in the warm ash, purring like a dynamo. We kept warm with typing, and with endless huge mugs of tea, warming our hands round the mugs before taking to the typewriter again. Pat used a hefty Olympia typewriter with golfball lettering. I used the remaining machine, an Olivetti. To help make the place warmer, John brought round some old red lino his parents had thrown out. It was that sort of place, like the home for Lost Boys — it's a wonder stove chimneys weren't poking up from the ground.

The Bookshop kitchen was set in a first floor bedroom, at the back. In the far corner was a small sink. The fireplace wall was a rich terracotta pink, with unusual curved sides and no sharp angles. The tiny bedroom fireplace and mantel were gloss red, painted late one night by Pat and myself when slightly drunk, with the paint we had just used for wall slogans. Pushed all together were a crockety leather sofa and armchairs which someone had discarded, a kitchen table, and a spanking new gas-oven, bought on HP by Pat to impress Rhoda, and out of kilter with everything else in the place. In the corner by the door the wall curved up in a whirl to the ceiling where the stairs continued their journey to the next floor.

Over the mantel was a small snap of Ben Bella, the FLN (Front de Libération Nationale) and NLF (National Liberation Front) flags from Algeria and Vietnam, a picture of a panda eating bamboo shoots, and a letter, pinned up like a testimonial, from a museum curator who had been expelled from the International Group for being in the BLA (Bureau of Latin America). It accused us of chicanery, treachery, quislingism, adventurism, and political buffoonery. At least, that's all I can remember, it went on for several pages in like vein and was much enjoyed.

* * *

On Christmas Eve I went to nearby Central Market to get tangerines, and Julian and Dick went off to steal holly and ivy from a vicarage. We all had food parcels from home containing Christmas goodies like plum pudding and cake. My sister called with a cockerel, but would never come in. Jill Westby came round on her bike and left a slab of their Christmas cake, which was decorated one year turquoise and orange, the colours of the Vietnamese Liberation Front flag.

Pat had the kind of personal hatred of priests and dogma that only a lapsed Catholic can aspire to, so he certainly didn't keep the festival and never sent cards. When the church carol-singers had their collection tin stolen, he rubbed his hands together. 'One in the eye for Baby Jesus,' he gloated nastily.

When the snow came the lavatory always froze, and we had to go out to it armed with kettles of boiling water, picking our way over the ice. The path to it sloped down in a twist and was particularly treacherous. The street-lamps cast pools of brightness in the dark, and snatches of animated Italian floated out before front doors closed again on the night. In winter the Bookshop was dense with latch-key children from late afternoon onwards, clustered round the paraffin heater, reading comics and chewing sweets and gum. A home from home.

The shop got warmer and warmer, moisture beaded the dirty dark-pink paper on the walls, and the mist of the night seemed to get inside, under the weak bare bulb. After about seven o'clock people started arriving for conviviality, from work, from university, from school and home. They were ushered past the comic-reading children, into the back room and up the stairs into the tiny kitchen.

Pat moved about like a whirlwind, he had a dynamism and enthusiasm that is rare in adults. His boundless energy fizzed into the air like seltzer. In his youth he had planned to train as a priest, and he claimed to have had a long and agreeable conversation about the merits of socialism with John Carmel Heenan when he was a parish priest, years before he became a cardinal. 'Well, well — you may very well be right. It takes all kinds to make our world,' ended the priest.

* * *

By the age of fourteen Pat had become a convinced anti-fascist. Near the end of the Second World War he had served as a wireless operator with the British Army in Germany. The Bookshop chess set was acquired as a trade-off for a pound of coffee in 1945 Berlin. It was inlaid wood with hand-carved pieces, and one of the pawns had chew-marks. 'They were made by one of those little creatures that are here and then gone,' he said tenderly. 'It made its tiny mark in the world by chewing this pawn, then it got distemper and pfffft — it was gone. It was a lovely little thing.'

A kid in the shop had stolen the black knight. Another kid had stolen a plastic one from his school's spare set to replace it.

One of Pat's favourite expressions was 'All they care about is their little piggy selves.' He would sometimes apply it to things most people would regard as valid to hanker after, such as a mate, a house, personal possessions. He didn't care about personal possessions. He only cared about making a difference.

* * *

Pat was pushing to be part of the Fourth International. It meant a great deal to him, to be aligned with the organisation set up by Trotsky in 1936, which contradicted the line of the Third International, set up by Stalin, which held that socialism is possible in one country. Trotsky advocated the theory of the Permanent Revolution, which was ongoing till the end of time; a revolution which would always have to be fought, even after socialism had become the basis of the state, and even after the withering of the state. Like war in heaven, it never ceased. You stopped the struggle only when you dropped dead.

He set up the International Group (IG) in 1962. Pat, Ken Coates and Peter Price were at the inaugural meeting at the Coop in Heathcote Street, and Ken Tarbuck came over from Birmingham. Everyone else was younger: students, apprentices and schoolboys mostly. I wasn't living in Nottingham then and came over with Richard, a schoolboy member of Derby Young Socialists.

* * *

In 1963 the Franco government executed the communist Julian Grimau. 'Every time those bastards kill someone we must ensure they don't just get away with it, there are repercussions,' said Pat to the group of teenagers around him. At night a bunch of us went with brushes and paint to the Lace Market, where the Spanish Vice Consulate was situated in a gloomy run-down building. We painted 'Grimau Lives On' and 'Down with Franco' and unscrewed the brass plaque — 'Vice Consulado de España' — then rang the Nottingham *Evening Post* to say a bomb had been planted there, as a protest against the execution.

* * *

John Daniels and Carol went with Dave Ablitt to see *The Legion's Last Patrol*, a film about the French Foreign Legion, and came away indignant at how it was portrayed. Pat was away so we wrote a leaflet about the brutal role of the Legion in Algeria, how they suppressed the heroic people and raped Algerian girl Djamila Boupacha. Then we gave out the leaflets to the queues of people outside the cinema. When they came back Pat and Ken were pleased. The music was high in the charts for weeks, but the film seems to have disappeared without trace.

* * *

Wednesday was the big day of the week. We worked flat out all day. Pat brought out a news-sheet on Wednesdays for organising the left generally, and more particularly for those working in the Labour Party. It was called *The Bulletin*, and as it became more widely circulated the name was changed to *The Week*. Typed and duplicated, it consisted of small articles and snippets from a variety of sources: the usual papers like the *Guardian* and the *Financial Times*, and in addition, a wide circle of people built up over time sent in snippets from various sources.

Hsinhua — the New China News Agency — came in bulky turgid reams every day and was invaluable, although you had to plough through masses of information all typed in capital letters. Also useful were the *Intercontinental Press*, from the Fourth International, on delicate tissue-paper sheets; *New Left Review* (it was the New Left people who chose the name *The Week*); *International Socialist Journal*, and others.

Jean did the student news. I did the American pages, going through *I.F. Stone's Weekly*, the (American) *Militant*, and the *Spartacist*. The US *Militant* backed Malcolm X not Martin Luther King, and its pages were full of the doings of Jimmy Hoffa — sometimes very formally James Hoffa — and the Teamsters Union. For a period I worked for Charles Butler, who supplied dresses to Marks and Spencer. He was an avid follower of stocks and shares, and part of my duty was to file the information which arrived daily. Of course, anything relating to South

African zinc shares or the like I'd take home to the Bookshop and copy, before filing them. Or Pat would give me a list of companies he wanted information on, and I'd find it at work. This duly appeared in *The Week*, as did all kinds of stuff the readers had sent in.

On Wednesday evenings a whole lot of people came straight from work to help collate and staple the paper together, address envelopes and stamp and stick them. The first person to arrive about four o'clock was always Andrew Rigby, a young apprentice printer. In his black duffel coat he was steadfast in support. We always finished with only about ten minutes to spare before the final post left at eight o'clock, and two or three people took the sacks to the Main Sorting Office while the rest of us staggered into the alley and across the road to the Bay Horse, completely exhausted.

The Bay Horse was a small packed pub, with two rooms and a thundering jukebox, old '50s style squiggly wallpaper and plastic flowers in sprays on the walls, and old ladies who drank port and lemon. We drank pints or barley wine. On darts nights it was thick with smoke and noise, and Nancy the Scottish landlady brought round big plates of free potato fritters.

* * *

Alfred Street Central, St Ann's, 1970. The Bay Horse pub is on the right. Photo: George L. Roberts

On Thursday afternoons Pat shut the shop for a couple of hours, and went off to see Chanchal Singh in his large dark grocery shop on Union Road. They talked politics fast and furiously, for Chanchal was the secretary of the Indian Workers Association. He supplied information about the subcontinent and sometimes translated short articles for *The Bulletin* from the Asian left-wing press.

* * *

From the Bookshop kitchen window you could see close-clustered housetops and chimney pots in rows of three, like tipsy crowned kings. In the winter everybody was in their houses with the curtains tight shut. But in the house immediately opposite sat a middle-aged man on a hard chair, his hand on an oilcloth-covered table. He never closed the curtains and he sat there night after night, doing nothing. We looked down and across, reluctant to draw the small curtains on him.

Jean wore a wonderful long tweed skirt to keep her legs warm. In winter I rarely saw my feet, my tights stayed on, black and dusty, and when I pulled at the toes dust rose like the smoking feet of a young devil newly come from hell.

* * *

Pat had left the Communist Party in the cataclysmic year of 1956 and that year his wife, Leonora, ran off with Rod. Pat, Leo, Rod, Rhoda and her husband Ken Tarbuck had been part of a bunch of young Communists then. They had a bond with one another that we didn't appreciate.

One winter Pat could be seen in close conflab with Rod Kreizman, who was preparing to join the IG. Rod was now married to Leonora and they had several children. In spite of this Pat still referred to her somewhat coldly as 'my wife' — for example: 'My wife, I see, has turned herself into a baby-machine.'

'Leo still agrees with you politically,' Rod assured him. Pat scowled. 'And I'm coming round to her way of thinking.'

* * *

One time in the cold weather Katherine came and dumped her furs in the chair and her diamond rings on the kitchen mantel, then spent an hour cleaning the kettle, rubbing and scouring and fetching it to a pitch of brightness that satisfied her. To tease her Pat said it had just sprung a leak, and she went a little mad.

'Oh! Pat, you old so-and-so, you should have told me… Oh no, get off Tom, naughty cat,' — she turfed Tom from the folds of musquash fur which he had happily settled into, leaving his ashy presence behind. 'Oh really — this place,' said Katherine.

She was John Varney's girlfriend, she came regularly and sometimes looked after the shop in an emergency. She was very good-natured and took what was dished out on the chin. 'When I looked after the shop on Friday evenings Pat told the children I was an Irish girl from Russia, that's why I wear furs, and if they were very good I'd speak Russian to them,' she said.

'Yes well he does tell dreadful lies. He told the children I was his stepmother,' I replied.

(Pat said, 'My father is a very old and very dirty old man, and he's married this young girl.' He screwed his face up, for the maximum of lurid drama, even seeming to lose his temper about it. The children stood agog. It was impossible to tell whether they believed him.)

* * *

Once a week Jean or I made a casserole with breast of lamb or pork hock. Now and again Pat did big fry-ups, throwing in everything in sight — apples, cheese, black pudding, sausages, marrow rings, macaroni, baked beans, peanuts — whatever was around. At weekends Julian came and cooked curry in his old school enamel OTC pans. He had been asked to leave his public school for organising a union. The curries he made were delicious, because he had roomed with Indian students at university and they had taught him cooking and gave him silk ties. Dick sometimes came round and cooked sweet potatoes and, once, goat. He had come from Jamaica, and had been in St Ann's during the first race riot in 1958. 'A bunch of them were coming down the street — I didn't wait to find out what they wanted! I ran down an entry and was over that wall into the next street,' he said, laughing and aghast.

* * *

On Sunday evenings after everybody had gone home Jean, Pat and myself played Chase the Lady, which shouldn't really be played by only three people as it leads to acrimony and spite. Of the chain of females Pat mooned over and induced to move in — Rhoda, Tricia, Caroline, myself, Jean — after some initial spats, they ended up making common cause and turning on him. This really served him right and underneath I think he accepted this too. Nowhere did it express itself more fully than when we played Chase the Lady in the Bookshop kitchen. With great enthusiasm and spite we ganged up. It was possibly a mild form of masochism in him.

Chase the Lady has lots of names, including Black Anne (after Anne Boleyn) and the nursery favourite Old Maid. It's the same game but with inverted perception.

* * *

One day Pat seemed particularly stressed. 'I've just had a phone call from Cordley Coit – he's coming round, so I shall have to listen to his ravings. I shan't get a damn thing done.'

Cordley Coit was an American photographer, a follower of Creative Vandalism. He was mad, but when you were in his company there was something totally disarming about him.

'I've come from Victoria Station,' he once announced with an air, 'and we've just painted it pink and silver.' The wonderful fantasy this gave rise to — the neo-Gothic all picked out in fairy-tale colours — was matched by a small piece of reality. Cordley and his art school friends had painted a single fluted pillar. Somehow the idea had got the better of him. Listening to him was often like listening to a small boy telling whoppers, from dazzling Victoria Station to him parachuting behind the lines in Mozambique with Stokely Carmichael. Although maybe it was true for all I know. He was generous with his time and bursting with ideas and was taking the photos for Ken Coates's book about poverty.

'Oh dear,' sighed Pat after the visit. 'I couldn't say anything — he's just so nice.'

Cordley and I always managed to spat. I liked him but his innocent arrogance irritated me. He'd swan into the Bookshop and say 'Just ring the newspaper and say you're from the St Ann's Students, Tenants and Residents Association, and read out this statement.'

'I'm not saying "students".'

At that time you would never have had students and residents in the same association — St Ann's regarded students with amused contempt — but it was part of a fantasy he nurtured.

'Okay, Cordley, I'm doing as you say for the greater good and not because you're telling me,' I said, dialling the number he handed over. When reading out the prepared statement I left out the word 'students' and he gave me a furious look.

A friend of Cordley's was Ray Gosling, the writer and journalist, a founder member of the Tenants Association. He sometimes came into the Bookshop with a little mongrel on a length of string. He stood for election for Council.

'Vote for a Madman' said the election posters and, it has to be said, he looked the part. Pat put up the poster in the Bookshop window; I took it down and put up the Labour poster. 'I'm voting for Fishface.' Fishface was Alan Johnson, member of the local evangelical church and Labour Party candidate. He was a well-meaning ineffectual guy and St Ann's Young Socialist meetings consisted of long rows between Alan and everybody else:

'No, we can't do that…'

'We're doing it, Alan.'

'No — oh dear, I really don't think — they won't let us, they'll close us down.'

'Who cares?'

St Ann's Ward Labour Party was a cabal of Wee Georgie Edwards, Wee Georgie's aged father and Wee Georgie's biker son who only turned up when his vote was required to swing things his father's way, and Alderman Frank Neale who had a wooden leg and right-wing opinions. There's no pretty way to put this, but Alan was basically a creature of these people. In spite of this, there was something staunch and decent about him.

One day, the 'Vote for a Madman' poster went up in the Bookshop window and came down half a dozen times. Then we had a row. 'He doesn't live round here, he thinks he can just come and lead everybody, it's just you and a bunch of art students — all four of them — who will vote for him, and everybody else will vote for Alan because he's Labour and he teaches at Sunday school,' I said.

'You're wrong — most people won't vote at all because it's the lumpenproletariat round here, in case you hadn't noticed,' said Pat.

In the evening Jean came from university and was appraised of the situation. She read the posters and announced straightaway, 'I'm voting for Fishface.'

Eventually both election posters were left up. Fishface won the election.*

* * *

The night before Jean's weekly tutorial she would clutch the book she was supposed to have read and take to her bedroom with vast quantities of coffee

* The council election was actually won by the Conservatives, but Ray Gosling's intervention split the vote.

and fags and panic, to read all night. In the morning she was so tired and so confused she often fell asleep and didn't go to the tutorial. So we cooked up a scheme whereby she read the first half and I read the same book from the middle onwards, to let her know what happened to all the characters. She said the first half of a book was more important because that's when everybody's character was established, and the rest of it was just their development and the working out of the plot. So, bending back another copy halfway through, I too sat drinking coffee, eating cheap chocolate and plodding through the action. *Mill on the Floss*, *Middlemarch*, *Mary Barton* — I started them halfway through and was thoroughly at sea. About two o'clock in the morning she'd come down into the kitchen and we'd swap notes, sit scoffing quantities of cinnamon toast — a practice instituted by Caroline — and I'd find out who all the people were I'd been reading about.

'Who the hell is Lucy?'

'Oh never mind about her, she's not important. Or is she? Does she come into it much?'

'Well I think Tom's in love with her,' — between bites of toast running with butter and sugar — 'Or maybe he isn't… anyway, they both die in the end, Tom and Maggie, the Floss bursts its banks…'

I could hardly care very much as I didn't know the characters from the beginning. In any case, I always had an inbuilt suspicion of the main female in Victorian novels, because the author was so anxious to show how innately morally superior she was compared to everybody else. Maggie Tulliver, Lucy Snowe, (I excused Jane Eyre for some reason) Dorothea Casaubon, with their lumbering consciences and marmoreal virtue.

After the natter and the toast we holed up again in our warrens to read some more. Jean didn't dare go to bed in case she wasn't up in time for the tutorial. Pat made her breakfast and I acquainted her with further doings of the characters, and by the united exertions of all three of us she got through the door.

Later the same day I'd settle myself with *I.F. Stone's Weekly*, mind reeling with acres of print, spinning with the change from Dorothea's marital pleas — 'I only want to be of use to you Mr. Casaubon,' — to burnings and demonstrations in Wattsville and New Jersey.

Jean became more and more peaky, and nobody was surprised when, halfway through the next term, the university psychiatrist advised she have a year off from her degree course.

* * *

Bridget, a Bookshop customer, was a red-haired bossy girl of eleven, on the front row when it came to stating her opinions or shoving in. She was the eldest in a big family; two or three of them were blonde, the others all brilliantly red-haired and for some reason referred to by St Ann's as the 'ginger-margarets'.

'It's another one of them ginger-margarets,' a customer said unenthusiastically, looking down at five-year-old Marie, who glared back at her from under a thick red fringe. Marie never spoke, she just glared a ginger glare. 'This is little Marie, isn't it Marie?' I said, trying to make the child feel better, not surrounded by blanket hostility. Marie scowled furiously at me and stuck her tongue out as far as it would go.

'Look – there's Marie,' I said to Julian, peering through the afternoon dusk in the children's playground as we went for a Sunday stroll. 'Cooooooeeeee — Marie! Hello dear.' The child didn't move.

Julian's eyes were sharper than mine — well, he wore spectacles 'Do you mean that dear little girl who's standing at the foot of the slide and spitting on the other children when they reach the bottom?'

'No she isn't. You always see the worst in people. Is she really doing that?'

Julian responded with a blast of sarcastic laughter.

* * *

Then came the last winter that Pat was there. In the New Year he was to move to London. As the Vietnam War intensified, so did our indignation. Photos were published of villagers — so poor they wore few clothes — fleeing the bombs dropped by the most powerful nation on earth. Our lives were consumed by the struggle against this brutality. It didn't look like war, it looked like an ongoing massacre. As it continued opposition was growing and the Vietnam Solidarity Campaign was founded in London. Pat was to work full-time for them, organising protests against the war.

'Do you want to come as well?' he asked me.

'Oh yummy, yes.'

'There's a condition. It's more suitable if I go down there married, it gets things out of the way. So I was wondering if — in the wider interests of the permanent struggle — you'd become Mrs Jordan.'

I was dumbfounded. 'But you don't believe in marriage. You've always said how idiotic it is.'

'Well, but this would just be for the sake of appearances.'

'I don't give a stuff about appearances and neither do you. Marriage is linked to petty bourgeois ideas of sexual ownership. And that's what you think too,' I insisted. 'I have nothing but contempt for it.'

'Yes, yes, but if you really had contempt for it you'd do this for the sake of something bigger than yourself,' he said.

'Well, I'd marry someone to save them from death, but that's about all. If you're so keen on the idea why don't you ask Jean?'

'Yes, I might do,' he replied.

Later on when I went into the kitchen to make coffee Jean was there and she whispered 'Guess what — Pat asked me to marry him — I couldn't make out why. Something to do with Vietnam.' We stopped whispering and stared at him when the kettle whistled and he came into the kitchen.

'Why don't you ask Jackie,' I suggested.

'I've already rung her,' he replied airily, 'and she says she might do.'

'Goody — I can be a bridesmaid then.'

He gave me a snotty look and poured water onto the coffee granules in the mugs.

Jill Westby came round on her bike to duplicate leaflets for a forthcoming CND demo. 'Is Pat all right?' she asked, a puzzled ruck in her brow.

'It depends what you mean — he's how he usually is.'

'Well it's just… er… he rang me up last night and asked me to marry him.'

At the next weekend school, as the wedding loomed, Pat and Jackie were incredibly chummy, ragging one another and arguing together. At one point they had an ice cream fight, after Pat took his teaspoon and lobbed vanilla down the front of Jackie's dress. She immediately retaliated by grabbing the strawberry ice on the dish from which Brian was quietly eating and plastering it on Pat's bald head.

'Can you use your own ice cream please, comrade,' Brian said mildly.

After that, it escalated, both of them dodged about the table, the other diners guarding their plates and looking over their shoulders as the pair hurtled by with shrieks.

'I've come a long way to have a serious discussion with Pat about my document on developments in the mining industry, and he's spent the entire weekend being silly with Jackie,' complained Chris Arthur.

'Just tell Chris Arthur, would you,' I said to Julian, 'that Jackie has had three love letters from,' — pause for effect — 'Chris Gray,' I announced grandly.

‘Chris Gray?’ he repeated, blinking and unbelieving, stunned. Chris Gray was expected to become a doctor of philosophy at Oxford.

Ho boo sucks.

‘Why should I tell him? Why can’t you tell him yourself?’ Julian said, reasserting himself.

‘Oh, he doesn’t take any notice of anything I say. And he thinks Jackie is silly.’

‘Yes, well, I suppose that’s based on the observation that she doesn’t mind people throwing ice cream down the front of her dress.’

‘Don’t be so stuffy.’

‘Silly?’ repeated Pat, when the complaint was reported to him. ‘Yes, well I haven’t read anything more silly than his bloody document about the mining industry. Just as though you tell workers that their industry should be wound down and their jobs lost because it would be good for their health. I’ve never read such bunkum in my life and I’m supposed to take his drivel seriously? I did the politically correct thing, in throwing ice cream I was demonstrating my total contempt for his document,’ he said, going onto the absurd and energetic attack.

The wedding was apparently off, neither of them mentioned it again.

* * *

The Bookshop without Pat would be a very bare place. But he was still going to come back and bring out the news-sheet once a week, from late Sunday to Wednesday, varying with the obligations in London.

As the year rolled to its close I was dreading Pat leaving. I didn’t see how we would manage without him. This was further reinforced by the time he had explained the intricacies of running the Bookshop — who would steal and whom I should let steal, either because they brought new stock in or because they were very poor; who to ban completely (and how would I enforce that?) and what books to put aside for which customer. I nodded intelligently and knew I couldn’t cope.

Romolo showed me the different comics, and I tried to remember them. ‘Jesu, you’re dumb. These aren’t just comics, they’re Marvel comics…’

‘Superman,’ I agreed, trying my best.

‘Superman? Aw him, he’s nothing much, he’s for little kids. There’s the Amazing Spiderman, Doctor Strange, the Incredible Hulk…’

‘Now this little girl doesn’t speak,’ said Pat. ‘She can speak — can’t you?’ The child looked back at him and didn’t attempt to reply.

'But she doesn't want to. So she'll come in and hand you the book she's finished reading and you must find her another one. She'll sit by the stove, and when she wants to go home she's allowed to take the book. That's because she's very good. She looks after the books and doesn't rip them,' he said praisingly. 'And she brings them back. No,' he half smiled and shook his head, 'we don't bother with money.'

The little girl — I never knew her name, but she had a younger brother called Pauly and lots of noisy shoving elder brothers and sisters — seemed remarkably self-possessed. She read books, not comics. She had chestnut hair, cut short with a fringe, and was aged about seven. She never uttered a single word, a laugh, a cry or any noise, but she would come up and hand me the borrowed book with a clear intelligent expectation of understanding and of being understood. I wonder what happened to her?

I opened the shop later and later. The customers seemed to take over. 'Where's Pat gone?', 'Where's old Pat, the old sod?' The Bookshop ticked over. A customer stole the bell. Another customer — a teenage boy — made us another one, an ingenious arrangement with a bent teaspoon which hit against the metal and tinged. But it often flew across the shop and customers scrabbled around on all fours to find it.

The gas meter was broken into — the only thing that was worth anything in the entire house. This left us with the money to replace.

'Never mind — we'll mend it when we get round to it. You can use the same shilling and keep posting it through and catching it,' suggested the gas man helpfully, lodging it nearby. Oh yes. What a good idea. The bill got bigger and bigger and there was one shilling there to pay it.

The Bookshop went more downhill than it was already. I was no good at getting new customers. Even Tom found somewhere else to live temporarily. Pat had drummed up business by stencilling leaflets advertising the books, and leaflets advertising a laundrette which paid him for it. So that brought in a little money and custom. Bridget offered to leaflet the streets. Romolo brought comics from home when the shop ran low — Marvel comics, much prized, from America. The pile of ordinary one penny comics grew rattier and tattier.

* * *

Spring came. The Bookshop wasn't as busy in the evenings, the children were out playing. In the kitchen one day Jean uttered 'Oh my God — look — there are children climbing all over the roof of that house.'

‘Those children — they live there. It’s a big family, they probably wouldn’t notice anyway if one of them fell off.’ I banged on the window but they didn’t hear.

‘What a very Malthusian way of dealing with their over-production,’ observed John Daniels, as we sipped coffee and watched them through the window.

* * *

On the Bookshop front door, behind the glass, was the big famous poster of a young Vietnamese boy making a speech of defiance before his execution. One night, very late and dark, there was a thumping and banging on the front door. Quietly, slowly, surreptitiously, I slid the bedroom window up and peered cautiously over the sill. Two storeys below a youth was staring as though in a trance at the picture, the street lamp shining on it. Suddenly he let out a scream of terrible anguish and threw himself against the door, repeatedly bashing the glass with his fist. I didn’t know what to do, didn’t dare go down to him. Pat would have known what to do, but he wasn’t here.

Early Days — London Demos

'Now girlies, there isn't enough hot water and it will take forever to heat more — do you mind sharing a bath?' said Nessie, running it for us. 'Here we are — lovely lovely French bubble bath.' We splashed about and squealed, flicked bubbles at one another as Nessie poured liquid into the steam.

Afterwards, frost on the window pane, we tucked into cornflakes and boiled eggs, me with soldiers, Jackie with matzos.

'It must be wonderful to live in London, everything seems to happen here — demos every weekend, lots of people at meetings,' I said to Tony.

'Oh, I suppose we live in a fool's paradise really, but we do our best,' he replied. We usually left for demonstrations from the Youngs' and made our way to the tube station, the trains crammed with demonstrators.

Under an unpromising sky in Trafalgar Square, the air full of moment, a woman's contralto voice came from the loudspeakers.

Men and women stand together
Do not heed the men of war
Make your mind up now or never
Ban the bomb for evermore

In a way they were more than just demonstrations, they were expressions of group solidarity. We reinforced one another in a mass and then went back to our lives, strengthened.

Demos that ended in Hyde Park slowed down as we reached the trees, people split from groups and formed other groups, girls released their hair from grips and repinned it or rewound scarves, stragglers adjusted footwear. One time a bunch of bright-eyed joyful Jewish girls linked arms and sang and danced *Hava Nagila*. There were lots of other people in the park as well on a Sunday afternoon, quite literally on soap-boxes.

There was a Committee of 100 sit-down in Trafalgar Square in the afternoon sometime in 1962. It was getting darker and we were all trapped in the Square. The police wouldn't let anybody out. In later years this was called 'kettling'. Jackie and myself had to catch coaches to get home and were fearful of missing them. Nobody knew what was going off because this had never happened before. Nessie approached a middle-aged policeman and started talking to him. Ron Bailey — a teenager then but afterwards he founded a housing charity — came up and started singing. 'I'll sing you a song and it's not very long, all coppers are ba…'

Nessie turned on him. 'You stupid thing, go away.' Then she turned back to the policeman with considerable aplomb. 'These girls need to catch their coaches, their parents won't want them travelling late at night and they have to be at work in the morning.' She put a proprietorial arm over each of our shoulders. The policeman nodded and said, 'Come on, come on,' indicating we were to go through. We left Nessie in the Square.

Victoria Coach Station — we hurried down the long road, known so well, I think we both made it to our respective coaches, I can't remember that we didn't.

* * *

Jackie was a big friend, we had met aged nearly sixteen at a Young Socialist week-long rally at the Miners' Holiday Camp in Skegness. She lived in Broadstairs and we exchanged long twelve- and sixteen-page letters. She joined IS (International Socialists) and often went up to London to demonstrations, and we met up at the Youngs'. The summer my parents asked me to leave home I went to stay for a week with Jackie and her parents on my annual leave. Her father had a position in the Coop and her mother had been a tailor. Jackie, their only child, was spoilt rotten. At the weekend we went to a Youth CND meeting in Canterbury. The weekdays I spent on Ramsgate beach, reading *Lolita* and sleeping in the sun, and Jackie collected me after work. Or I stayed in and heard Mrs Taylor's stories of Jackie's childhood. Her mother was lovely and asked me to live with them. 'I have one mad girl, another one won't make much difference.' In the evenings I went to various meetings with Jackie, or visited her political friends, and met the people I had previously heard of in her letters.

One time after a demo the Youngs were away and Jackie and I stayed at Tony Cliff's. He was the leader of the IS and he lived near the Arsenal football ground — the telephone number was London, CANonbury — with his wife Chanie Rosenberg and their (then) three children. Everybody on the left, of whatever faction, liked Tony Cliff, even if they disagreed with him politically. Even Ken Tarbuck, who could be quite factional, asked warmly about him when he knew I'd stayed there. They had briefly been political allies at one point. 'How's his little girl? She was a lively little soul. Lanila.'

Cliff was a small round man with lots of curly grey hair and a friendly manner. He kept saying 'These pop singers, this music — we should be part of that.'

'When Lannie was about six,' he told us, 'she argued there was a God. "How do you know?" I asked her. She drew a picture of an eye. "That's how I know. Because you can't explain an eye." As a matter of fact it's wrong, the eye can be explained rationally. But it was a good argument from a little girl.'

On the Saturday evening Gus Macdonald called round for a chat, mostly about the YS. He was the Scottish delegate to the YS national committee, and had just moved to London to produce *World in Action* for ITV. His girlfriend was Teenie, one of the Shoreditch Belles. They were three girls in Shoreditch YS: Joanie, Nonnie and Teenie.

After the weekend there was a mass exodus early on Monday morning with Chanie — I think she taught English at the local grammar — Lannie and Donny all going off to school. Tony Cliff was a house-husband when it was all but unknown, he stayed home and wrote documents and looked after the baby. He sent Jackie and me to the shops early to buy food, and then he made us spaghetti Bolognese before we left. I made a strawberry mousse. 'Oh, but you must make one for the children,' he insisted. I felt bad but hadn't time, I had to be on the train because I was due back on the switchboards at 2.40pm — a split shift, my friend Chris was working the morning shift for me. It was very expensive to do this but we didn't pay each other, I then owed her the time.

* * *

Demonstrations were mostly in the spring and autumn. Sometimes at the Youngs' my head would be in a bowl of steam and covered with a towel, Nessie putting in some pungent oil — I think it was Friar's Balsam — to help my asthma. Nessie and Tony lent me Max Eastman's *Why You Should be a Socialist*, an American copy. I read it and took it back a couple of months later when I stayed there again.

* * *

'I'm going to fight, fight, fight to save the party I love,' Hugh Gaitskell shouted back at the Labour Party conference which had voted in favour of unilateral nuclear disarmament. Putting himself at odds with conference guaranteed internecine warfare on a large scale and deep

deep loathing towards Gaitskell himself. 'Fight! Fight! Fight!' — the words went everywhere, with Gaitskell's photo. There was a row at *Young Guard* editorial board because this had been on the front cover, giving the first impression we agreed with him. At a Young Socialist rally Jackie and Gaitskell's wife had a fearful row, two tiny females spitting hatred.

Gaitskell died unexpectedly and mysteriously of a virus. We were all embarrassed, I remember feeling red flood into my face because we had detested him so much.

'It's terribly sad when anybody dies, whoever they are,' Nessie said firmly.

* * *

Och, och, get oot the Holy Loch,
Get oot the Holy Loch,
Get oot the Holy Loch, och och och,
Och, och, get oot the Holy Loch,
For we dinna want Polaris.

From a demonstration a favourite IS man and I danced the length of the long road from the tube station to Ranelagh Gardens with a carton of milk ('There's no milk, you'll have to get some,' said Nessie) singing protest songs in the middle of the night, the key to Nessie and Tony's flat jumping up and down in my pocket as we skipped. Once there, we had the place to ourselves.

The 1960s were a much more innocent time than is supposed now. We spent all night together in the low bed, usually shared with Jackie, chatting and kissing and falling asleep. If we had had sex it might mean I'd have a baby, and then he would have to marry me. So we didn't. It was his choice.

He had been in the old MCF (Movement for Colonial Freedom) which preceded the Anti-Colour Bar Campaign and Anti-Apartheid. A schoolboy at the time of Suez, he went on demos against it with his classmates. 'It became very violent, we took marbles to roll on the floor to bring down the mounted police.'

'But what about the poor horses?'

'Yes, and what about poor us with them charging at us?'

He had the brief fad then for wearing a watch with the face on the inner wrist to protect it.

Next day we took the tube into London and he took me for breakfast, because he seemed in charge. Another time we went to see *Hiroshima Mon Amour* at the local cinema.

* * *

One demo Jackie and I went to I remember well. She must have been staying at the Bookshop because we left together from Nottingham. We rushed to Victoria Station to catch the London train — 'We're going to the big demo against the Vietnam War,' we said. We were cutting it fine, and the ticket officer rang down to the platform to ask them to hold the train. We ran down, down, down the steps, CND badges in place and long hair flying behind. The stationmaster had waited with his whistle poised. When we reached the platform — 'Here they are!' — the uniformed staff broke into applause, and the stationmaster hurried us into the carriage. We hung from the window waving as the train pulled out, and the porters and staff waved back and cheered, and even the stationmaster gave us a smile.

I've never forgotten it and I could cry when I think what has happened to our darling old railways. They served the British nation, men devoted their lives to the service of the railways, the Queen travelled by British Railway, and travellers came before profit.

* * *

Julian's parents invited me to spend Christmas 1963 with them, and he was to meet me at St Pancras Station. I was looking forward too to meeting some of his friends from Eltham Young Socialists, and he had theatre tickets to see the new show, *Oh! What a Lovely War*.

I travelled down on Christmas Eve, wearing a lovely coat, dark green with a circular lucca lamb ruff. I'd bought it that autumn from Willsons in St. Peter's Street, Derby. It had cost more than a week's wages — six guineas. I'd saved for months, and it felt momentous handing over such a large sum for a coat. Leaving it behind for slight alterations, I collected it the following week. 'That coat — it's a model coat, it was sold with the wrong price tag. It's twelve guineas,' said the lady assistant. Seeing my face fall — I couldn't possibly afford it, six guineas was bad enough — she said, 'No dear, we can't take it off you, you've paid for it.' She sent a girl upstairs and took the coat from the hanger. 'The manageress wants to see you in it — put it on.'

The manageress came downstairs and smiled and said, 'You look lovely, my dear,' and kissed me. So I travelled down to London in a stunning twelve-guinea coat.

'You look adorable — just like a kitten,' Julian greeted me. This was strange, he was often quite rude.

Julian's parents lived at Eltham. His mother, the eldest of five lively sisters, was tall and had been rather beautiful and had married well, and quite rightly wasn't the slightest bit grateful. She seemed in control and told her husband and son what to do. His father, a patient and agreeable man, worked for the Woolwich Building Society. He looked at his wife with a mixture of amusement and wonder at what was coming next and was obviously still greatly in love with her. They had a comfortable home, well-built in the 1930s. The large light sitting room was spoiled by a big picture of a gloomy modern crucifixion, given by Julian to his mother on her birthday. She had gamely hung the thing up. 'I expect I shall get used to it,' she said uncertainly. It obviously wasn't her taste.

'If you ever give me a picture like that,' I said when we were alone, 'I shall hang it face to the wall.'

On Christmas Day his mother gave me a bottle of Goya Black Rose and I gave her a copy of *The Group* by Mary McCarthy and his parents a big box of Thornton's chocolates, which could only be bought in the Midlands then. There was a traditional turkey, and his parents reminisced about the war. Afterward in the kitchen, while I helped with the washing up, his mother said, 'This politics is all very well, Sylvia, but where's it going to get him? Look at the education he's had.'

'Where's it supposed to get him?' I replied sulkily.

In the afternoon his aunt and uncle and girl cousins Renata, Simona and Edwina came for tea. We played games as the day darkened, and everyone conspired to let the little one win at cards. On Boxing Day evening he took me to see *Oh! What a Lovely War* in its first production. I'd never seen anything like it in the theatre. It was dazzling and tragic and stayed in my mind for years. Another day we went to Greenwich to see the Cutty Sark, and I met Julian's friends Tony Stone and Bill Vester in the pub, and they told me about their YS branch and its doings.

* * *

In my room at the Bookshop I put down rush matting, bit by bit. The Youngs had this all over their flat. I left Caroline's parchment walls but painted the fireplace wall dark midnight blue. A battered cupboard, a bookcase and a divan bed was the only other furniture. From a colour supplement I pulled a big picture of Aubrey Beardsley's Salomé, bearing the head of the Baptist on a platter, and fixed it to the midnight wall 'Hmmm — poisonous, isn't it,' remarked Pat. It was. And I have no idea now why I liked it and wanted it there. Perhaps it chimed with something nasty in me. Young people can be quite cruel.

The midnight wall was copied from Geoffrey Worthington's flat. Julian and myself often stopped at his place after a demo or conference. It was on the top floor of flats in Lisle Street, very central, and was a hub for young gay men (I don't think the word 'gay' was in use at that time, people said 'queer' or 'poof').

Geoff was in the International Group, the YS and Paddington Labour Party. He had been to one of those expensive schools where pupils can do as they like and this was reflected in his behaviour. He seemed to be here, there and everywhere and up to all sorts. He was a NUPE union representative, he also had a medical degree and practised psychology part-time and was involved in all kinds of schemes, part-owning gay clubs and up to his eyes in machinations in the YS and Labour Party.

His cousin John, in the Royal Navy, stayed over when he was on leave, as did a succession of young sailors. John would turn up late at night looking smart in his naval uniform and with a bottle of whiskey.

Somewhere in the flat was a room containing what was referred to as 'Frank Ifield's bed', reportedly used when the famous singer and yodeller stayed over. It was frequently alluded to, but I never saw it.

Geoff was small and slight, canny, and with a deal of self-assurance. You were in the presence of a weighty person. We acclaimed him with enthusiasm when seen in the crowds on demonstrations, with his dark glasses. Behind them were amused brown eyes, reddened in the daylight if he removed them. He turned up with one of those tiny colossally expensive cameras, ready to catch untoward police behaviour.

Tea and toast at Geoff's on the morning after a demo was great fun; he always knew the gossip and what was going on. He got on wonderfully well with the elderly prostitute in the flat below, but was in a long-standing bitch with the nightclub on the ground floor, pursuing a lawsuit against them for disturbing his beauty sleep. Actually it was several floors below and he didn't care, but he was hoping for a big payout — 'A nice lump of compensation will help the old coffers, my darling.' Eventually, I believe, he was awarded it.

His flat was a pad for moving London in the 1960s, a haunt of sailors and Marxists, conjubilant with gossip and ongoing schemes. Yet in spite of the gregariousness which he delighted in and engendered, there was something very lone about Geoffrey.

At one point the word went round — Geoff was involved with a woman, she was staying at his flat and he was refusing to have anyone else there. Whoever was she? Everyone wanted to know. Snippets of information leaked out, bit by bit. She was Grace, she was Latin American.

'This mustn't go any further,' said Pat. It didn't, but it's so long ago now it wouldn't matter. She was from the Latin American Section of the Fourth International, and she was on the run. It wasn't clear whether from a government or another left group — Posadas perhaps (it was the tail end of the internal bust-up with the Latin America Bureau). Her safety was paramount, that's why Geoffrey wouldn't let anyone into his flat.

One of the last times we saw him was at Hythe Summer Camp, where the amalgamation between the International Group and the Revolutionary Socialist League took place, which he had fought tooth and nail. He kept saying, 'Oh God, now what are they doing?' — obviously with no great expectation of it being anything intelligent or to his fancy.

He seemed to drop out of the IMG (International Marxist Group), the merged group, well, most of us did eventually, and I don't know that he went earlier than others. The gay movement was becoming vociferous so maybe he became more involved. Julian was inclined to think not. He believed Geoff liked the gay world the way it was — in the midnight shadows. Who knows?

We didn't hear from him again, apart from a possible allusion on BBC News a few years later when the AIDS crisis hit. 'A mysterious Dr Worthington is giving free advice and medication at a Paddington Clinic for AIDS sufferers,' said the newsreader. Vague. It might have been someone else. But it was likely to have been Geoffrey.

* * *

After Jackie left home she went to stay with relations in London, and then moved to Kilburn, and I went to stay with her. It was a multi-occupied IS household but I only saw Esther, who was in the same trade union as Jackie, the other tenants were away. Jackie and myself had lots of rows, but not about politics. As she said, you work with whoever is around. No row was as intense as when she told me she'd given away Helen's cat to a laundrette. I didn't know Helen but was incensed on her behalf because Jackie said she was still calling it. 'It wasn't your cat, it wasn't your business.'

'She leaves the bloody kitchen window open for it and then clears off for the weekend. When she gets back it's "Has anybody seen the cat?". Now it's getting fat as a pig in the laundrette.'

* * *

We went to visit Highgate Cemetery. Wandering around in the disarray and ruined angels and fallen columns, we picked our way through tumbled stone and waving grasses. So this was it. Marx's grave. 'Workers of all lands, unite.' We sat there thinking of Marx, who devoted his life to trying to make things better for his fellow human beings.

'We should have brought flowers.'

'We'll bring them next time.'

Of course there never is a next time. There was a second-hand bookshop near the cemetery and I bought a copy of *Moll Flanders* and a postcard of Marx's grave. I put it in the book as a marker and it's still there.

The Ring

On the Bookshop kitchen shelves was an old tin with green circles on, which held sewing materials — cotton, needles, small scissors and an old rolled-gold wedding ring.

Pat surmised it had been left behind by Rhoda, when her marriage had split up. She and her husband Ken Tarbuck had rented the two rooms on the second floor, and when he stormed off after a row Rhoda had had a brief affair with Pat, before doing a moonlight flit with the two small Tarbuck girls, leaving behind a tom-kitten, a hamster, two goldfish and the ring. Pat was upset by Rhoda's treachery, but pleased and diverted by the animals. He continued to open the shop and write documents about the political situation, and young females calling themselves names like Kitten and Tiger dropped in now and then to sympathise with him and clean the kitchen. Kitten was a young plump nurse who, when her shifts permitted, turned up unannounced and scrubbed and disinfected and then read him her long and dreadful poems on world peace and why we should get rid of the bomb. Christine — I mean Kitten — was a lovely girl with a nice nature and a soft heart, and on one of her scrubbing essays she found the ring where it had lodged between floor and skirting-board, probably when Rhoda had taken it off and thrown it at her now ex-husband.

Pat had a history of sympathising with young distraught females, who often moved in. After Rhoda there was Tricia, then Caroline Volkov, deeply ashamed of her White Russian traitor relation whom nobody had heard of anyway. 'She's very sensitive about it, I have to keep reassuring her that nobody would care, even if they'd heard of the notorious Anna. They accept you for what you are here. But she is such a vulnerable person...'

Caroline might have been sensitive but she could be bossy and difficult. 'I don't see why you need to use my room. You should have made proper arrangements, Sylvia, it's not my fault if you haven't anywhere for your meeting. Is Dave Ablitt going to be there?' she demanded.

'No, he's been banned,' I lied. Dave and John Daniels Junior had got drunk together in the Bay Horse one weekend. John had lurched home but Dave banged on the locked door of the empty Bookshop, and then climbed onto the wall and followed Tom the cat up the slanting scullery roof, and was right behind him when he latched the kitchen window open with his paw. Then he'd crawled upstairs and into Caroline's bed when she wasn't there and been sick in it.

When she moved in Caroline was livid at having to decorate because Tricia held a party before she left and the merry-makers had scrawled slogans over the walls. She papered old newspapers on the ceiling — she said it would keep the room warmer in the winter. I helped her paint the walls a parchment colour. Then she painted shelves and stood a mixing bowl on them. 'Oh what a lovely bowl,' I said.

'It is, isn't it?' she agreed warmly, stroking her hand about its curve.

It was the same mixing bowl that was in every kitchen of my childhood, with curvy capacious white inside, set in a beige figured dish, there since time immemorial. As it sat on Caroline's shelf its curves seemed slightly askew. I'd never seen it like that before. I remembered it with pudding mixes beaten in, with apple pieces floating in water, and all manner of incipient food in the process of becoming, in those kitchens of mother and aunts and neighbours. But Caroline was the first person in my experience to use the bowl as an idea rather than as functional. After she obtained her degree she left to teach weaving in Rimini and Brian Lynam had her room for that summer, before he moved in with Rhoda. I joined the household gradually, as I became more friendly with Pat and the Bookshop crowd.

The summer of 1963 I was in Kingsway Mental Hospital, after taking an overdose. Pat and the comrades visited often, and he wrote a long letter most days. He signed me out — my parents refused to — and I returned to the Bookshop.

That autumn Pat went to address the University Socialist Society, known as Soc. Soc., and met Jean. Days afterwards he was still mooning about the Bookshop, saying how deeply sensitive she was and what an emotional state she was in. It was extremely peeving, he wanted to sit up late at night talking about her instead of about me, and finally it was arranged she would move into one of the tiny Bookshop rooms piled on top of one another. 'She needs to get away from all the restrictive bourgeois behaviour that surrounds her.'

Jean was tall with big dark eyes and taut with nerves. She smoked like hell. She was in her second year, reading English. Once a week the three of us put ten shillings each into a tin, so Pat could pay the Coop milkman to deliver milk, cheese, butter, eggs, bacon and potatoes.

This saved us the bother of shopping and meant there was always something to make a meal. Jean was sent to get her own Coop divvy number, and once a month all three of us attended the Coop Individual Members Section (IMS) meeting. It was mostly ladies there, they were very friendly, they wore fancy flowered hats and — unlike the Labour Party — treated Pat with great respect, as though he was a professor or something. Mind you, he was on his best behaviour, and was rather gallant to the ladies. The IMS passed a resolution calling for Nottingham Coop to buy Yugoslavian wines and jams, and trade with Eastern Europe and socialist Algeria. So Nottingham Coop stocked lovely plum and cherry jam from Yugoslavia, and tins of scrumptious stuffed aubergines from Bulgaria. At the next meeting we planned a resolution on Algerian wine.

After initial mutual suspicion, Jean and I became firm friends. 'Oh I'm so glad you're living here too,' she pronounced. 'Because I'd far rather be thought part of a *ménage a trois* than that I'm living with Pat.' We weren't a *ménage a trois* but I understood what she meant.

We hadn't much respect for our elders, even the ones on the left, and we were very dismissive of Rhoda.

'Brian Lynam was round this afternoon, advising us to go and see Rhoda if we have any personal problems — the idea of it!'

'Huh — she's the last person I'd ask. Look at the mess she's made of her life.'

Pat heard us with a shake of the head at our callousness. He still had a soft spot for her; she turned up sometimes to type for him, declaring he was the best friend she'd ever had.

'Poor Rhoda. She's had a lot of things against her. I knew her when she was your age — she had just as many hopes and dreams as you do.' Rhoda reminded me of Lana Turner — blonde, slight, highly sexual in a restrained suited manner.

Katherine came too and cleaned the Bookshop kitchen as the fancy took her. Her boyfriend John Varney was a schoolboy at High Pavement. The first people from Nottingham I met were four High Pavement schoolboys — John, Chris Holmes, Dave Collins and Tony Taylor. We were at a Young Socialist school at Skegness. 'The point is,' said Tony urgently, 'do you believe the universe is finite?'

'I don't know.'

'No, you don't know, but what do you believe?'

'I think it's infinite,' I said randomly.

Chris and John were having a noisy pillow fight on the beds. Tony's father, Ted Taylor, was a leading light in the Cosmo Club, a bunch of quarrelsome old men who met at the Coop in Heathcote Street. Although Tony came to the first meeting of the International Group, after he left for university we didn't see him. Chris went off to Cambridge but always came back. Dave went to Fircroft College and then Merton. He too was in the IG from the start. John was East Midlands Business Manager of *Young Guard*, and I took over when he went to teacher training college. He still went out with Kathy and was very active in the International Group and the Students' Union.

Katherine and John had been going out together for some time, and when they went to conferences they shared a hotel room. You couldn't do that then unless you signed the register as a married couple and sported a wedding ring. Katherine pulled a face at the ring in the sewing tin, and turned one of her expensive rings round the other way.

Jean began to see Dick Skyers, who was older and married, and one of the two black members of the Group. Jean and Dick often drove off to the Yorkshire coast where he had been stationed during the war, in the RAF. They walked the beaches on the east coast and then feasted on hot teacakes in little out-of-the-way bed and breakfast places, and stayed the night, and Jean took along the ring for this part of the trip.

* * *

It was the Labour Party Annual Conference, and Julian booked a room for Mr and Mrs Atkinson, so I tipped up the sewing tin again and took the ring. When we arrived Julian found his union, the National Union of Labour Student Organisations (NALSO), had booked him into a single room in an expensive hotel, where many MPs were staying. He was loath to abandon this splendiferous accommodation. A bunch of us left him at two in the morning, still arguing in the hotel lobby with other Young Socialists, MPs, and a couple of Hungarian diplomats. While he was thus engaged I was sharing the double bed booked for Mr and Mrs Atkinson with Tony Stone, a sympathetic friend.

'My girlfriend went off with a sword-swallower,' he said.

'I liked her,' I replied. She had been at the last school.

'Yes, she was okay. But how could I compete with a sword-swallower?'

Tony Stone was in the same Young Socialist branch as Julian, and I liked to hear all the chat about Eltham's doings. Eltham YS started all meetings with a rendition of their favourite pop song 'Duke of Earl'. All members stamped their bovver boots and chanted in voices as bass as they could make them:

Dook Dook Dook Dook of Earl,
Dook Dook, Dook of Earl,
Dook Dook, Dook of E-aaarl Oooooo…
When I walk this world…

They passed a resolution voting it the greatest record of all time.

The previous Christmas an Eltham store had unknowingly employed a Marxist Santa from the YS, who had illicitly loaded his sack and ridden up and down Eltham High Street in a horse-drawn carriage throwing not just sweets but expensive toys to passing children.

'What about the Marxist Santa?' I prompted Tony, eager to glean any more details.

'Oh you heard about that?' he laughed 'The branch felt that act of appropriation was in keeping with the true spirit of Christmas.' Then, 'What on earth are you wearing on your finger?'

'Oh that —' I took it off and looked at it. 'It's not mine. We all wear it. Put the light out now.'

In the middle of the night we started scrapping and had a row and the light snapped back on. Afterwards he didn't snitch to Julian — whom I told anyway — but advised him I wasn't a very nice girl. And after that he got a new girlfriend called Diane and we all became friends.

Another occasion I wore the ring was completely different. There was a strike at Raleigh. Two women started a wives' anti-strike group.

'That bloody woman — she's interfered before, in the Rolls-Royce strike. She poses as being non-political but she's actually a rabid Tory,' spluttered Pat. 'It's a pity that we can't expose her…'

We cooked up that Jean and I would go to one of the meetings, to see how many people turned up and what happened, pretending to be wives of strikers. Out came the ring again and I put it on my finger, and Jean kept her gloves on. It was late autumn I think, it was dark when we went on the bus to Raleigh Works. Three women were at the big entrance on Radford Boulevard. They were the only ones there and one of them was a journalist from the *Evening Post*. A quite small lady was very pressing.

'We know the men want to go back to work, but the union won't let them,' said the woman. 'We must put pressure on them. It's up to you, you know you can do it, you can help to end this dispute…' We didn't say much, both of us totally out of sympathy with what was scarcely a meeting, unless three people chatting in a works' reception area counts as a meeting.

Pressed to say more, we couldn't keep up the pretence any longer.

'Well, actually we don't agree with you, we support the strikers,' one of us burst out. I think it might have been me. The journalist pushed in. 'So what are you doing here? You're pretending to be someone you're not. And are you married?' she demanded.

'Yes —' flaunting the ring — we didn't want to look like total liars. Boy, was I glad to get on the bus back to the Bookshop. But they could hardly pretend now they had mass support.

'Here, can I borrow that ring?' demanded Jackie. She had started an intense affair with Dave Ablitt, they were both nuts about each other, although they rowed a lot as well. She was on her way to a conference. Once again the tin was turned upside down.

'Where's the ring everybody borrows?' enquired Bonnie, when she moved in. When shown the completely ordinary thing, her face beamed.

* * *

Another occasion Jean and I were involved in was nothing to do with the ring, but gives a flavour of the time. The Young Socialists had called a big demonstration at the House of Commons against youth unemployment (at this time it was nowhere near what it later became). We were to lobby our MPs directly on the subject. I went off sick from Charles Butler, the factory where I was working, and so did Jean from the Tourist Information Centre where she was working during her year off university.

We marched and then Jean and myself filed in to speak to our MP, Peter Tapsell. We were rather nervous, he was a Conservative and we didn't know how he would behave. He turned out to be handsome and sympathetic and received us amicably.

'You see, it's so distressing for young people if they can't get a job, it undermines their whole view of life…'

He nodded encouragingly 'Yes. Oh yes, I do see that…' he smiled as he listened then interrupted one of us mid-flow. 'Just tell me one thing,' he said kindly. 'Are you married?'

We sniffed at the parliamentary air suspiciously. 'What's that got to do with it?'

He smiled gently at us and said 'Oh I think you'll find once you are married all these things that are upsetting you so much now won't matter at all, you'll forget all about them…'

'What!!!' we shouted back. Then he pulled out of the conversation, abstracted himself, obviously relegating us to the slot: unmarried and barmy.

This couldn't happen nowadays. But back then a female and her views weren't authentic unless she was married.

* * *

One day I was travelling to London on the train in the same compartment as Anne from Leicester. She was totally non-political but resembled all of us then, with a short skirt and long hair and a friendly open smile. Our ideas were instinctively similar too, she believed in what was known as Free Love and invited me to night-long parties, and we swapped addresses although in actual fact we never met again.

'My friend Terri is getting on at the next stop. She's travelling to see her boyfriend, he's a soldier, he's coming down from Catterick...'

When Terri got on Anne said, 'This is Sylvia, she has the same ideas we do, she doesn't take any notice of parents and she's going on a demonstration in London.' Terri grinned and glittered goodwill at me above her fur collar, and we were soon chattering and exclaiming over each other's lives. I brought out the ring and told them about it. They uttered cries of delight, and on an impulse I gave it to Terri, although she didn't need it. She took it with enthusiasm and put it on straight away. We spent the rest of the journey sharing anecdotes. Terri was to get off the train at Luton, and we went with her into the corridor. As the train slowed and stalled, Terri jumped up and down excitedly. 'Oh I love you, I love you, hurry up,' she said into the air. When the train finally stopped we wrenched open the door and pushed her out, she fell straight into the soldier's arms. They hugged one another with happy faces. And that was the last of the ring.

The Labour Party

Nature — so benign — has drawn a merciful blank over the meetings of St Ann's ward Labour Party as far as I'm concerned. Jean and myself went to weekly YS meetings, but didn't often go to the adult Party.

The political scene in Nottingham in the early 1960s was still reeling from the Popkiss affair, a corruption scandal involving local government and the police of so serious a nature it had been in the national news night after night.

The only meeting I remember was the one to support Ken Coates. At this time there was an ongoing campaign by the Labour right — the agent Len Maynard and co. — to expel Ken from the Party. There was a big meeting of St Ann's ward to discuss it. Most of those who came — from the right and the left — didn't usually turn up, they were mobilised by each side. The meeting was held, I think, at the Union Stewards Club on Gordon Road. Pat, Jean, Dick and myself went and also Vimie from the Glasgow faction. There were lots of people on the right too and it was an immensely disagreeable meeting. I can't remember which way the vote went — against Ken I think. There was also a big rowdy meeting at Lenton — Ken's ward. He wasn't there but Geoff Coggan led a spirited defence on his behalf. We came out in force to support him. I have no memory of what was said at the meetings, just a general feel of how acrid and spiteful they were.

Although we didn't often attend ward meetings we did canvass when it was required, before the May Council elections. On Sunday mornings we met at the bottom of Robin Hood Chase, about half a dozen members. As Jean, Pat and myself neared the small group Alderman Frank Neale whispered — but loud enough for us to hear — 'Trotskyites.' Mike Sillitoe gave us a big friendly grin, he wasn't allied with them and sometimes came round to the Bookshop. George Edwards nodded tersely. Of that group only Alan Johnson came over and spoke to us. Because Alan was in the YS there was a strange loyalty there. Alderman Neale looked the other way and wouldn't speak to us.

This happened on a number of occasions and God knows why we didn't say 'Okay, if we're Trotskyites (the 'ites' revealed the hostility) and not fit to speak to, you can do your own canvassing.' But we felt it was important to have a Labour rather than a Conservative administration. It made a difference to working people. Of course eventually people did stop canvassing *en masse* and the Labour Party stopped winning elections. And the more difficulties it got into, the more it witch-hunted.

In the early 1960s Harold Wilson accused some Labour members of being 'Trotskyites in bedsits'. This seems the reverse of the 'Putney Debates' on suffrage in the Civil War (Colonel Rainsborough: 'I do believe every man in England should have a vote'). The subliminal message of Wilson's words was that those living in bedsits shouldn't be allowed to vote. This was odd, because Wilson in many ways was a kindly figure, he had a soothing, healing voice and attempted rapprochement with the separate elements in the party, especially when compared to other leaders — later, Kinnock and Blair. Wilson's immediate predecessor, Hugh Gaitskell, was totally loathed in young left circles, with a detestation I've never encountered again, not even of Thatcher.

'He has a saving wit, I suppose,' remarked an amused Paul Foot of Harold Wilson, who was speaking at a YS Skegness Rally.

'There you are,' quipped an unfazed Wilson later, when he was Prime Minister being pelted with eggs at a public meeting. 'Under a Labour government eggs are cheap enough to throw about.'

Wilson was difficult to dislike, he had a warm northern-inflected voice and seemed on good terms with everybody.

'We'd like to thank George — where is George?' he asked expansively of a crowd of supporters, like Wilfred Pickles, wanting to share the crowd's attention with a helper.

And Wilson did respond to pressure over the Vietnam War. He refused to send British troops. Resolutions were being passed in constituency Labour parties all over the country, as well as unprecedentedly large demos against it. Wilson never faltered from giving verbal support to LBJ but he always refused troops. He withheld tangible support. In reality this was perhaps more important than if he'd intoned the NLF's demands over a microphone. It must have infuriated the American government and its supporters here and I believe — with no evidence whatsoever — that's probably why Wilson was got rid of.

The RSL/Militant group in Liverpool were totally loyal to Labour and for their pains were constantly vilified and eventually expelled after they gained control of the council. There is no other place on God's earth that resembles Liverpool — why shouldn't they have a Trotskyist council?

* * *

Of the right-wingers in St Ann's who voted for Ken's expulsion, oddly enough he had a soft spot for George Edwards, in spite of his politics. This was since Ken had seen him at a Council bash sitting miserably in a corner, bent over an orange juice.

'Hello there George, how are you? Aren't you drinking?' he called warmly.

George leaned forward, bitterly surveying the merrymakers getting sloshed at ratepayers' expense, and said, 'It's not right, you know.'

Most of the members who voted against Ken I think didn't understand his ideas. They were mystified by words like 'Trotskyite', which acquired in their world a patina of evil, to be resisted.

* * *

Ken made an enormous contribution to the struggle of the working class, he was full of energy and enthusiasm. He and Tony Topham, a lecturer at Hull University, started the Workers' Control conferences. 'Workers' Control', if you think about it, is sensible. When I worked for the GPO, our union, the Union of Post Office Workers (UPW) believed in and gave out pamphlets about workers' participation, and there was always union representation on management committees. That workers involved in day-to-day work should have a say about the overall situation seems common sense. The interweaving of power strengthens society, and makes it less vulnerable. At the end of *Hamlet*, when Fortinbras strides in, the state falls to him like a ripe fruit because the key figures are dead, they have destroyed themselves and they had no powerbase. Had the society been strong from below it would have saved itself.

Who are those against Workers' Control? And why are they against it? And it should be faced head-on — without the trades unions the Labour Party doesn't exist. When Tories and their ilk point out, 'The unions are behind Labour,' instead of trying to wriggle out of it, it should be acknowledged and argued through. There is nothing to wriggle out of. As Frances O'Grady has said 'There is no cleaner money than trades union money,' — it comes from the pockets of working people. If you don't believe in the working people of this country, then you don't believe in this country. On society, Ken always quoted what was said among miners when he was a miner himself 'It's not fairation.'

* * *

In the 1950s the Labour Party had youth sections. They were junior adjuncts of each individual local Party and didn't exist as a national organisation. But there had started to be an upsurge in youth activity generally — in music, fashion, the arts — and the Labour Party decided there must be a national youth Party organisation.

The first annual conference of the Young Socialists (YS) was at Easter in 1961. George Brinham from the NEC presided. He was right-wing but sympathetic to the young.

The first speaker was Liz Thompson from Wigan. She complained that their motion (on housing) had been disallowed by the National Executive and she was being blocked as a delegate. A noisy conference voted overwhelmingly in her favour, that she should be heard. (When eventually she was expelled from the Labour Party for being in Keep Left, she took the 500-strong Wigan branch out with her, but this was several years later.) We passed resolutions on nationalising the banks and scrapping the nuclear deterrent. Derby YS sent three delegates — Alan Mullarkey, George Roberts and myself. Alan's wife Alma, about to have their first child, came too, and we all stayed at the Bedford Hotel.

The conference was exciting and it seemed important — a huge dark hall bursting with stroppy youth. Alan was voted the first national chairman. The only other speakers I remember were Jean McCrindle from Scotland, and Paul Rose from Manchester. They both received standing cheering ovations. After the conference ended large sections of it joined the Aldermaston march outside London.

The conference was at Belvoir Hall. 'Aye, and a right bunch of busy little beavers you've been,' remarked George Brinham, who seemed amused and avuncular rather than intimidated by the youthful intransigence. In spite of his political views he was quite popular with the YS, but he was not to see another YS conference. He was killed by a Young Socialist. He had invited the teenage youth back to his home and made advances to him. The boy had panicked and hit him and ran out of the house leaving the doors wide open.

The NEC weren't sympathetic, they felt he had brought shame on the Labour Party. Dave went to a YS national committee meeting — he was the East Midlands delegate — and came back enraged at the adult NEC's attitude. 'That bitch Alice Bacon and Bessie bloody Braddock and that bastard Reg Underhill,' he spluttered. They had vetoed the YS passing a motion of sympathy.

* * *

It was Alan Mullarkey who first introduced me to Pat Jordan. 'Come on, I'm going to take you to meet the most dangerous man in the East Midlands,' he said (This was before he became 'the most dangerous man in the country' — copyright *Daily Mail*, 1968).

We went on a bus to Nottingham and crossed the city on foot. Alan seemed to know where he was going. When we arrived I saw that it was a tiny shop in a backstreet, with lots of comics. Alan talked to the owner, Pat, who was pleasant enough but made no impression on me.

We didn't get to know one another until the CND march one Sunday from Nottingham to Ripley. Friendly with Nottingham YS members, I'd stayed at Katherine's overnight to be at the start of the march in Slab Square. We all set off in good humour, it was a sunny day in, I think, late spring, to walk to Ripley. All the Sunday schools were out, waiting to wave and cheer us on as we passed. Everyone was in high spirits, CND members were there from all over the East Midlands, and people they hadn't seen for ages. At one point a man with a guitar sang protest songs. As we walked the fourteen miles I became friendly with Pat Jordan, chatting away under a big banner.

When we arrived several hours later at Ripley marketplace there was a big public meeting calling for nuclear disarmament. A man called Peter asked me out. The following week he took me to see *Midnight Lace* at the Gaumont. Then he gave me his card — he was an architect with Derby Borough Council — but I didn't ring him. He was nice but he was twenty-eight and that seemed quite old. The next I heard Sylvia Bardiger had run off with him.

* * *

Dave Ablitt was an apprentice at the ROF (Royal Ordnance Factory). He was active in his YS branch and usually represented them at conferences and on the national committee. An acolyte of Pat Jordan, he was a drinking companion of Paul Waplington, whom he revered. Dave positively enjoyed making the middle-class and the delicate squirm. He spoke of 'my ale' and 'supping' in almost sacred tones. ('No I can't go, I'll be supping,' or 'We were legless,' he'd gloat). His world was peopled by 'owd ladies wi' fruit in their 'ats.' There were plenty of middle-aged and elderly ladies then who wore straw hats decorated with fruit, mainly cherries. Perhaps they had worn them as girls.

Dave traded convoluted insults with Pat as a matter of course, usually greeting him, 'Hello turdonovich.' In some respects, he was Pat's right-hand in the YS. Pat wrote articles in the *Bulletin* under the name of Dave Windsor, which many assumed was Dave Ablitt. Pat acknowledged with a laugh that he had chosen the name deliberately for that reason.

* * *

Pat listened to our concerns. He was even-tempered and encouraging, but there were times when he suddenly became a seething knot of fury. One such occasion happened when a comrade didn't attend a Labour ward meeting to push a resolution on Vietnam. Pat took the matter absolutely personally. 'All I know,' his eyes screwed up with boiling temper, 'my mates in Vietnam are fighting for their lives with guns in their hands and he can't even be bothered to get off his arse and turn up to a meeting. How are we going to build anything? How are we ever going to help them?' The fact that he took it so personally I think made it even more real to us.

* * *

Begone! dull care, I prithee be gone from me,
Begone! dull care, you and I shall never agree.
My wife shall dance and I will sing,
So merrily pass the day,
For I hold it one of the wisest things
To drive dull care away.

In the mornings I often moved about in the kitchen singing snatches of songs learnt at school — 'Westering Home', 'Golden Slumbers', 'The Ash Grove', etc. When I broke into 'Begone Dull Care' Pat wore a specially acid expression. 'Do you have to sing that?'

'You prefer "Golden Slumbers"?'

'I didn't say that. My wife used to sing it when we had a disagreement. She'd go on singing it over what I was saying so she couldn't hear me,' he said tartly.

This made me laugh — the picture of young Communists Pat and Leonora at home squabbling over the saucepans about Stalin's latest utterance. Leonora came from a solid Communist family, she was sent to nursery with hammers and sickles embroidered across the yoke of her little smocked dresses, and initially she stood by the Stalinist line after Pat had junked it.

Those who felt it was a good thing so many members left the Communist Party in 1956 were probably the same people who castigated the ex-CPers being allowed to join the Labour Party. But where else were they to go?

* * *

An entrist wouldn't be my first word of choice to describe Pat Jordan, although in a way that's what he was. But I think he would say he went where the struggle was — first the Communist Party, then the Labour Party. There was no fight for workers' rights in the Conservative Party,

There's a lot of talk now about entrism as a tactic by Trotskyists plotting to enter the Labour party and take over. Much of it is rubbish. The young Trotskyists I knew were in the Labour Party first. We sang the 'Red Flag' as though it was a hymn. Nottingham North YS, for example, was jam-packed full of schoolboys. Some of them became Trotskyists — but after they were members of the Labour Party.

There were those who could be described as entrists as well as Pat: Ted Grant of the RSL and maybe Harry Selby in Glasgow. Yet both of these had a fierce loyalty to Labour.

There was an International Group meeting once a month at the Bookshop. Ken Tarbuck came over from Birmingham, as did two other comrades in touch with Pat over a long period of time: Alex Acheson came over from Leicester and Martin Flannery from Sheffield. Were they entrists? Well, they were Trotskyists, yet they were both secretaries of their local ward Labour parties. I always thought of Alex and Martin as supremely stable; upstanding, courteous, measured in their responses and unlikely to fly off the handle or be abusive. They were Proper Grownups. Alex, a teacher, wore tweed jackets and highly polished brogues on his big feet. Martin was in charge of an English department at a big school, he was rational and pleasant, with a hint of Yorkshire irascibility in his voice. He later became a headmaster, and then a highly effective MP for Sheffield. (Years later, in 1983, the Falklands conflict loomed. Thatcher was strident, Michael Foot called for military action, as did the *Sun* newspaper and even *The Militant*. Everybody had gone mad. Over the radio from the House of Commons came loutish baying from Tory backbenchers, and then the stern headmaster's tones of Martin Flannery calling them 'a set of bloodthirsty hooligans.')

One person who was definitely not an entrist was Ken Tarbuck, an open Trotskyist since he was a young man. He had been in the old RCP (Revolutionary Communist Party) years before, and never in the Labour

Party. When I worked at Derby Telephone Exchange I was sent on a week's Directory Enquiries course at Birmingham. Whilst there Ken and his new wife Barbara asked me to tea one evening. Barbara was a small social worker with naturally curly hair, and she smiled as Ken said, 'Like you, Barbara's in the Labour Party, and she's hoping to convert me. But we'll see.' Then he said 'Once a week we give ourselves a little treat, and we've brought it forward a day as you've come. We have pineapple creams from the Coop.'

It was a very nice tea, and the pineapple creams were special — pastry cases with layers of pineapple jam and mock cream (being a war baby I prefer it to real cream), covered with pineapple water icing. After tea Ken fetched out the old Trot newspapers from the 1940s and 50s with articles in them by him as a young cadre. Jock Haston featured large. 'Of course, I knew Jock Haston, he was a very impressive comrade,' said Ken. 'But he joined the Labour Party eventually.'

When I got back to Derby I went to the local Coop looking for pineapple creams.

* * *

7th February 1963
[postmark Margate]

Dear Sylvia,

Thanks for 'phoning me whe you were at your sister's. I'll split half the cost if you have to pay for the call. Did you go and see Nessie & Tony during your holiday? I do hope so as I know they would have been delighted to see you.

At our last YS meeting I was nominated as delegate for Conference, like a silly fool I declined and nominated Len Bishop instead. But I thought he was the best person, he's had the pleasure of having once been interrogated by the NEC for his connection with Keep Left and knows more about the ending of the League of Youth and the forming of the YS than I do. He's not a Keep Lefter any more, but a good leftwinger, so for political reasons I'm glad he's representing Ramsgate.

Our YS resolution for conference is on housing. It didn't meet with too good a response at the GMC, because it advocated municipal estate agents, and one of the leading members is an estate agent and a crook into the bargain. But our Secretary Agent said it was a splendid resolution, and if it doesn't appear on the agenda will want to know why. We're jolly lucky to have such an agent.

Also at our last meeting we started a series of lectures on 'The Growth and Outcome of Socialism', being given by NCLC lecturers, who seem pretty left-wing. The idea is to give political education to the branch. I'm hoping to get Tony Cliff and Tony Young to give talks. The general attitude of the branch is good, and I think within a few months Ramsgate should have a jolly good left-wing militant branch.

On Saturdays we're starting to leaflet and canvass for the YS, spending alternate weekends on YS and YCND (to be constructive and keep our members active and interested).

On 23rd/24th February there's a Southern Region weekend school at Tunbridge. Richard Marsh (that nit — remember him?) is speaking on 'The Next Labour Government'. It should be interesting to know what his views are. Also what a position in the government he's allocated himself. About six from our YS are going, paid for by the Party.

The weather here is perishing cold. Last week the sea was completely frozen. A seaside town in winter is so depressing. One wants to sit huddled up in front of the fire all the time. But Socialism isn't achieved like that, and one has to put on a brave face and venture out into the beastly cold to further one's beliefs.

I should see you at Scarborough if all goes well. At the moment I'm having my monthly row with my parents. They keep on at me, how mad I am spending my money on going to Conference. In fact every time I mention I can't afford something I get shouted at. In fact my father says I can't go. I've got to save like fury and not mention Conference and not go to London, until YS Conference at Easter. But I should get there then, by hook or by crook.

Sincere wishes,
Jackie

* * *

The Labour Party Conference was almost always held at a seaside town — Blackpool, Brighton, Bournemouth, Scarborough — every autumn. I only went as a delegate once, from Derby YS. Dave went from Nottingham YS, Julian went as national secretary of NALSO (National Association of Labour Student Organisations) — the left-wing student union. The NUS was non-political then, concerned only with organising Rag Week and the like. Ken Coates was everywhere, sometimes as a delegate from Nottingham Trades Council, sometimes not a delegate at all. Brian Simister went as a delegate from the Trades Council. For most of the 1960s, for years, the leader of Nottingham Trades Council was Lionel Jacobs, a Jewish Communist who'd fought in the Spanish Civil War. In later years it was Brian.

One Conference merges into another for me. A whole bunch of us went from Nottingham IG to the Scarborough Conference. The first afternoon we met up with people we knew from other constituency parties and assessed the lie of the land and traded experiences over the year. We had brought copies of *The Bulletin* with us, specially tailored to conference resolutions. This was before *The Week* was produced on a daily basis during Conference week and renamed *Labour Briefing*.

We strolled towards the sea. It was sunny but cold and only a few of us had brought swimsuits. Julian, Carol, and Dave (in leopard-spot trunks) held hands and ran together shrieking into a roaring wave. Then we went for fish and chips, as you always do on the first evening at the seaside. The first night we were busy making contact, discussing the resolutions, and planning how to get them passed or how to amalgamate them. Different caucuses were held in various rooms. Labour conferences then weren't the manicured PR events they later became under Kinnock and Blair, they were fierce and vibrant, delegates really believed in their resolutions and wanted to see them passed, hopefully on the way to becoming law if Labour became the government. The idea that their resolutions might be thwarted by other members enraged them. Some delegates had been waiting a year to verbally savage certain MPs. Fist fights weren't usual but not unknown. Even when you went to the beach and held a seashell to your ear the enraged roar from Conference could be heard. The MP for Grimsby, Austin Mitchell, reputedly sent a holiday postcard back to his constituency: 'Wish you were here. The blood's lovely.'

The leadership contest after Gaitskell's death was held at Scarborough, with Wilson, Brown and Callaghan standing. Non-political people liked George Brown because he was often drunk, but when sober he was extremely boring and extremely right-wing and was heartily disliked by the left. (Belper YS, a bunch of schoolboys at Strutt Grammar led by Don Holland, David Hallam and Simon Cutts, said when they were old enough they would vote Liberal rather than for George Brown. We had cordial relations with them, they took *Young Guard*.) Anyway, Harold Wilson won, which was the best choice. Afterwards we gave Conference a miss and got buckets and spades and went down to the beach and began building a great sandcastle, a complex of four towers and ramparts. It was so big we stood inside its grounds, dripping wet sand slowly to make castellated tops.

Brian was ticking away as he worked, 'This castle is a socialist castle, I'm making the walls extra secure. No-one can come in if they aren't socialist.'

Julian pointed out, 'Socialism in one castle. You sound like a secret Stalinist, comrade.'

It took hours before it was finished. We collected pretty shells and Jackie and I decorated the castle walls with them. Eventually, tired but happy, we drew back, elated at the magnificence of the castle and its keep.

Off we went for a celebratory drink, and to discuss the new leader and what had happened at Conference. Then we wanted one last look at the castle and returned to the sea wall. Silently we watched the sea slide forward, quick and then quicker. It came running up the beach and around and then into the castle. It stormed the ramparts and went swirling into the bailey. Silent and suffused with melancholy, we left it to its fate.

The Ghosters

At one point there was a vogue for frequenting a pub on Saturday nights known as the Ghosters, in Lenton. It stood on a totally bare stretch of road, surrounded by the rubble of the houses where its customers had lived. The landlords, Stan and Myra, were waiting for the brewery to give them another pub. In the ghost area, as a way of sustaining their trade, they served drinks throughout the night, with the blinds pulled down fast. It was a gloomy place, there was no music or loud noise, and in the fullness of time was itself to be demolished, so the brewery had spent no money on it for ages.

On the battered dismal counter stood a large glass jar of Myra's pickled eggs, 10d each. About two in the morning would come a furtive knock at the window — it was the policeman on duty, come for a sit-down, a warm at the fire and a free beer. This was hardly corruption, but an honest appraisal of the landlords' situation. How else but illicitly were they to make a living?

There were three rooms and they could be filled with quite a lot of people. In the winter there was a fire. In the back room, if the conversations rose above a certain level, Myra would appear in the door and say sternly 'Shhhh — Sandra's asleep,' and point to the ceiling. Sandra was their daughter, she was a nurse at Nottingham General and depending on her shifts, if she was off-duty her rest was sacrosanct.

Round the walls was a set of old framed photos of Stan and Myra in top hats, Myra had high-heeled shoes and fishnet tights, balancing a conjuror's stick. She was a big lady, and I think their faces had been transposed onto other bodies.

'Mmmm — how do you make these pickled eggs, Myra?' I asked.

'That's my secret, love.'

The rooms were quite small and were often filled with Peter Price, Ken Coates and people from the university, like John Daniels Senior.

* * *

At the end of the long deserted road was another long stretch, Park Road. The official address on every copy of *The Week* was well-known in left circles — 54 Park Road, Lenton. In fact, nothing to do with *The Week* was ever done there but it was felt to be a more respectable address than Dane Street.

It was Peter Price's house, he lived there with Maggie and their baby, Emma. Before I'd had any contact with Pat Jordan, I'd been taken to a

CND meeting there by Sylvia and Maurice Bardiger, from Derby Young Fabians. Maurice was an optician and Sylvia was his attractive wife. She wore expensive clothes and Helena Rubinstein's Noa-Noa, smoky and intense, you can't get it now. They often gave me lifts, and l shared the backseat with their little mongrel dog Georgina. They were glamorous, and when we arrived at Park Road it seemed glamorous too. There were large William Morris prints on the whitewashed walls:

When Adam delved and Eve span
Who was then the gentleman?

— muscular Adam and large Eve with apple and long twisty hair wound about the twisty tree.

It was an old building, by itself on the bare road. Ken Coates lived upstairs then with Marina and their baby twins and they put in a brief appearance at the CND meeting, where people had come from all over the East Midlands, sitting on the floor and wherever they could.

Peter was older than Ken and Pat, jovial, bearded in an Ernest Hemingway fashion, with a booming voice and bonhomie. He was a teacher, heavily involved in the acting world and all kinds of campaigns, as well as being a Labour councillor and a key member of the International Group from the beginning. When I bewailed owing him money for petrol on a trip, he said 'Forget it, I'm rather flush at the moment,' but I felt guilty.

'Oh don't worry — you know Peter, he's the uncle of the world,' Julian said. And that does somehow seem to describe him.

* * *

One night I had a row with Pat at the Ghosters — I can't remember what about — and he went off somewhere with some people. Finally at about three in the morning the rest of us staggered out onto the road that led nowhere except into endless rubble, everybody breaking up and going their different ways. It was found that Pat had left his briefcase, which was handed to me to take back to the Bookshop. Staggering over the rubble, it seemed heavy; then very heavy. I was still livid anyway and drunk and suddenly l didn't see why I should take his briefcase back. He needn't think I'm looking after his fucking briefcase, he just uses me — pick his briefcase up, type some stencils urgently, run about after that sodding shop... l went muttering on. Serve him right if it was lost.

Uttering a loud cry I hurled the thing into the midst of the night and the dereliction, and felt a whole lot better.

The next morning — or rather, later the same morning — I woke and realised with horror what I'd done. There was a heavy feeling in the pit of my stomach. I didn't know how I would explain it. Pat didn't explode when I told him what I'd done, as I had thought he would. The situation was too serious for that. He wiped his plump hand backwards over his bald head. 'Oh Christ, mate. That contained the internal documents of the United Secretariat. Stuff about Algeria and God knows what else.' We were both absolutely sober with the seriousness of the situation.

'We'll have to go and see if we can find it. Can you remember where you flung it?' Well, I couldn't really, but back we went to Lenton.

After fruitless kicking and searching across the acres of land, scattered bricks and weeds, we had to acknowledge the briefcase had gone. 'Well. That's it.' He kept saying don't worry, it was his fault, his responsibility. We walked half-heartedly back to the Bookshop in the silent Sunday streets and were just having a miserable cup of coffee when the telephone rang. It was Ken. The briefcase had been found by a retired police inspector who had been walking his dog in the early morning. He had picked it up, looked inside and seen Ken's address and telephone number. Naturally, our relief was somewhat mixed at hearing this.

Pat decided I should go to collect it with Brian. He always assumed that he looked too sinister himself or not quite respectable. He rang Brian and arranged for him to meet us.

'Now what have you done?' Brian chided me, although his warm Cheshire voice had the effect of soothing people, which is why he was often asked to smooth things over with the wider world.

Pat lurked in the next street, and we walked up the pleasant leafy avenue and rang the bell of the semi-detached house. An old-fashioned policeman answered the door, how I thought of policemen when I was a child — moustached and friendly and faintly fatherly, earnestly wishing to be of help. 'I knew straight away they were important documents, that's why I made enquiries immediately, I knew somebody somewhere would be worried,' he said.

'Thank you very very much, it was so kind of you.' The briefcase was handed over in the stained-glass vestibule and we touched hands, the smells of Sunday dinner floated out — imagination painted in the Yorkshire puddings and the gravy in its boat and maybe apple pie afterwards — part of an easy-going traditional life, that life we didn't have any more, a world I'd left: respectable, kindly, decent.

Brian swung the briefcase at Pat, and went off to his Sunday dinner too. 'Now come on, you can have anything you want,' Pat urged, delighted at the outcome. 'Just tell me what it is.' This never worked but anyway it was a game we played.

'A proper Sunday dinner,' I said, 'with gravy made from vegetable juice and roasties and roly-poly afterwards.'

'Hmmm. I'm afraid the exchequer won't run to that. Tell you what — when Chan's opens this evening we'll get warm Jamaican patties. And I'll take you to my parents for lunch next Sunday. They have all that kind of stuff there.'

As we sauntered through the deserted streets wrapped in that special Sunday feeling, centuries of quiet laden into it, it never occurred to me to wonder why Pat automatically assumed there was something disreputable about himself. He gloried in it, yet he couldn't do anything about it, even if he'd wanted. We wandered across the felled land squabbling and making plans, like a cross fairy and a bad elf left out in the rain while the family is inside with the fire and the food.

* * *

The first year I lived at the Bookshop Pat promised to take me to the church of St. Mary the Virgin to see the wild cats that lived in the grounds there, which people fed. We walked through the deserted Lace Market early on Sunday morning. Across the churchyard and grass, it was silent and we saw no cats. Rows of empty dishes stood behind the church railings. Pat opened a tin of cat food and produced a spoon. 'Tom won't mind.'

'I think he will.'

'Well, we won't tell him.'

Just as we were leaving there was a quick swish of a tail behind a tombstone.

* * *

On Sunday afternoons Granville Stone rode over from Belper on his motorbike to deliver copies of the Cuban paper *Granma* to Ken Coates and others. Granville supported Cuba and the Viet Cong but had no time for the Labour Party. By the age of twenty he had led two successful strikes at Calverton Pit. Later he was sacked from a Foundry and Coronet Tool Company in Derby for recruiting members to a trade union.

We always tried to support strikes. When the nurses were about to take industrial action, Kitten came round, without her Lysol but with another nurse, Sylvia, to duplicate leaflets and chat with Pat.

'You will come to talk to us, won't you?' urged Sylvia, a West Indian girl with pretty roses in her cheeks. Pat had promised them I'd go to the hospital and speak of the work-to-rule our union, the UPW (Union of Post Office Workers), had run a year before. Afterwards I had expressed uncertainty to Pat.

'Yes, you must go. You'll find it easy. Just talk to them. Taking industrial action is one of the most important things you can do, it gives people hope. They learn in struggle. It shows how workers are needed, they start to blossom when they see this and no longer feel the passive plaything of outside forces, they have at least some control over their lives. You must do your bit, mate.'

It's true. It's exciting, your heart beats faster — you are engaging with the forces that make our world turn.

'When you act collectively it's life-enhancing, uplifting, both a transformative and a restorative experience.'

* * *

The bread strike affected everybody, but I can't remember that we involved ourselves. People were buying flour instead of bread and made their own. At the Bookshop Jean made bread thick and stiff and nutty and it made a change.

During the long seamen's strike of 1963, Dave's elder brother John, a sailor, sent in regular reports to *The Week* from Hull.

A big one was the busmen's strike, against Nottingham City Transport. We went down to public meetings in the Square and turned out leaflets, and Pat was up and down to Chanchal Singh's grocery store to take the leaflets and get the latest information as there were quite a few Sikh busmen. In fact they formed the backbone of the NCT hockey team, which was rarely beaten.

Paul Waplington drew a fantastic sketch of a conductor with his large hand open and big pennies on it, which was put out on a leaflet with something like 'Just a few coppers'. A big march wound through the city centre, periodically a loud cry went up at the front:

'Who are we?'
'— NCT.'

A transport strike is always disruptive, people had to walk to work and it went on for a few weeks but was finally won by the busmen.

* * *

Paul Waplington played in a brass band that turned up on May Day. He was a lace draftsman and an artist and a big mate of Dave Ablitt's, in fact he tutored Dave in some of his most obscene expressions (which will not be reproduced here). Julian said 'Dave is gifted at creative obscenities of course, but you haven't heard the master,' meaning Waplington.

He painted and sketched — landscapes, working people, lace workers, miners and Nottingham streets. He started to go abroad quite a bit to paint, returning to Nottingham every so often. 'Back to the licensing laws and bloody Merrie England,' he said gloomily.

May Day, Hyson Green by Paul Waplington
(courtesy of www.paulwaplingtonart.com, original painting in Sheffield Museum)

* * *

Everyone was jubilant at the success of the Cuban Revolution which we all felt part of.

In early 1962 Pablo Armando Hernandez, the poet and, I think, the cultural attaché at the Cuban Embassy, came to Nottingham with Robin Blackburn to speak at the university. Afterwards he spoke to Katherine, he was part Irish and asked about her family. I was in Derby and was disappointed to miss it. I put a copy of *History Will Absolve Me* with its cover drawing of Fidel and the Cuban embassy stamp up in my bedroom like an icon. There was a long poem about Fidel and the Revolution by Lawrence Ferlinghetti. I typed it out and Pat duplicated it and we gave it out as a leaflet. We didn't bother about copyright, we supposed the poet wouldn't mind.

John told Kathy off for 'monopolising' the Cuban. She shrugged her shoulders and defended herself: 'He stayed with Ken so he was probably fed up with politics and just wanted to listen to drivel.'

* * *

Leafleting, public meetings and demonstrations; raffles and benefit nights were held to raise money for the Vietnam medical fund. Picasso sent a painting from his Blue Period, to be auctioned to help VSC funds. Locally, Bob Gregory and Bill Keeton turned Bob and Judy's kitchen upside-down making marrow and ginger jam, which couldn't be easily obtained then and Bob said would be a big earner for little outlay. John Daniels Junior, an apprentice printer, made the jam jar labels for nothing. The end result was advertised in the *Guardian*. I don't know if it made much money but it certainly made a lot of fuss.

The American pages in *The Week* were increased to cover all the many reports coming in from rioting burning cities. 'From our reporter in Watts, Luther Pepper,' — a made-up name to put with the amalgamated and précised accounts gleaned from *Spartacist* and (US) *Militant*. It was elided from Drs Luther King and Pepper, and sounded as though we had our own black journalist on the spot.

Living at the Bookshop, you were liable to be asked to type documents any time of the day or night. When banging started on the shop door I would stagger from bed and shoot up the sash window, putting my head into the midnight street.

'It's urgent, comrade. Can you cut a stencil, the working class need to know this as soon as possible…' It would be something somebody had decided to write over a conflab in the pub. After a while I got pretty ratty when knocked up in the night. Or there would be a telephone call: 'If we come round now, comrade, could you type us a stencil? It's very urgent…' Anything to do with the Vietnam War or if there was a strike, I regarded it as a duty. If Pat was in London only Jean could operate the duplicator, and if she had gone home in the holidays it was no good. But eventually her visits home became shorter. There was so much to do.

The life of Nottingham in the 1960s would have been considerably depleted without the Coop. Its main building in Upper Parliament Street went on and on, with windows to rival Rackhams in Birmingham. There was the Coop Arts Theatre in George Street. The Coop built a large complex of meeting rooms, ballroom and cinema — the Coop Film Theatre (now the Broadway) — between Heathcote and Broad Streets.

Just down from the meeting rooms was the Normandie Café, where we often went. It was spotlessly clean and gay with red and white gingham tablecloths, and the food was simple and reasonably priced — egg and chips, beef sandwiches. The proprietor was Spanish and very welcoming, he often sat at one of the tables with his family.

Derby Coop had its own dairy herd and creamery, I'm not sure about Nottingham. The dray horses were stabled down London Road, and also the drays themselves which were increasingly motorised and without horses. Tricia, Dave Collins and I went down to book one for the YS float on May Day. Tricia always knew what to do. She got a great nodding head representing Harold Macmillan from somewhere and the float was entitled 'End Tory Misrule'.

* * *

'Carol is so kind-hearted,' said Pat. It was true. She was a librarian at Strelley, but the staff were moved about and when she was at Nottingham City Library the word went round IG members, they took their overdue library books back and she didn't charge them. John Varney had so many books out it saved him pounds.

* * *

The university Socialist Society (Soc. Soc.) had other members in the IG as well as Jean. The most forceful was Pat Fryd. She always wore black with high buskins and had fair, rampantly curly hair and smoked black Russian cigarettes. There was Judy ('She's magnificent,' said Brian Lynam appreciatively) and Dinah who came round to the Bookshop now and again on her bike, with a biscuit tin hanging by string from the handlebars. It had holes punched in because it held her pet mouse, which she had coloured pale pink with cochineal to resemble a sugar mouse, leaving a white patch on its belly so it could breathe through the skin.

'Tom's never seen a pink mouse — let's show him,' Pat suggested.

'No! — you shan't show my mouse to Tom.'

'Aw, Tom'll give a loud shriek and run off,' said Bob, showing how well he knew the cat's ways. Dinah came to duplicate Soc. Soc. leaflets, mostly about the Student Union or anti-apartheid, and afterwards stayed to have delicious little chats with Pat about her new boyfriend.

'Well, I think he's a fine comrade, he has a wide appreciation of the arts too, and he's very fond of you.' He smiled encouragingly and Dinah glowed.

* * *

Tony Southall, Pat Fryd's boyfriend, was also in the IG. He was at Cambridge, and at the end of the Cuban Missile Crisis he banged on the Bookshop door about 5am and got Pat up. Thinking the world was about to be blown up, he had posted a letter to his tutor saying exactly what he thought of him and his ideas. Now it wasn't the end of the world after all he was rushing back to Cambridge to try to intercept the letter. 'He was in a right state,' said Pat. 'He asked to leave his stuff here and went off to catch the early train.'

After obtaining their degrees Pat and Tony were married in Harpenden and everybody went. The bride wore a gold lamé cocktail dress with a corsage of freesias and the groom a black velvet jacket. There were no speeches but dancing and chatting and food from the buffet. Near the end there were cheers as the bride's father, the local Labour Party agent, proposed a toast to the happy couple. The marriage didn't last long but everybody said it was the best wedding they had ever been to.

* * *

Since the days when the Bookshop had sheltered students there was a Bakelite box resembling a chocolate bar stuck on the wall of all the rooms at the back. It was a Rediffusion box. Pat paid the rental weekly (4s 9d I think). He insisted we hear Alistair Cooke's *Letter from America* on Friday evenings, and we often listened on Sundays too.

'He's a right-wing journalist who is always worth listening to. You mustn't miss it, it has all kinds of insights.' We listened to the news on the hour and *The World at One* with William Hardcastle. Pat tuned in to a *Book at Bedtime*, especially if the reader was Gabriel Woolf — a favourite of his.

Suddenly we all started listening to *The Archers*, people collided with each other to switch on rather than switch off.

'A strapping Irish navvy has put Jennifer Archer up the duff,' announced John enthusiastically. This was greeted with a great cheer and so much glee you'd think a Trotskyist demand had been met. The strains of *Barwick Green* floated about every day over the documents, the duplicator, the waiting typewriters.

Factions — and Faction Fights

Pat sorted through the post, ripping open the brown envelopes with gusto, light-heartedly discarding the bills inside. Then he handed me a large mug of tea and took another one up the stairs to put outside Jean's door. 'Tea, comrade.'

I reached over to see if Jackie had written, and found among assorted newspapers, periodicals and letters a heavy typed manuscript, *The Way Forward*.

'Oh, an RSL document — my favourite.'

Pat, back down from thumping on Jean's door, looked patient and grinned. He knew it was a dig at him.

The RSL were the Revolutionary Socialist League. They had developed from the RCP — the Revolutionary Communist Party — and as such were a direct descendant of Trotsky's Fourth International. This pristine lineage impressed Pat like mad, he hankered after it, but had certain political disagreements with them, mostly to do with their method of work, which was entry work inside the Labour Party of so deep a nature they were indistinguishable.

Anthony Sampson, in the first edition of *Anatomy of Britain*, wrote something like, 'This is a group so secret that its activities aren't visible to the naked eye.' This caused multiple chucklings from Pat. In subsequent editions it was deleted.

The Young Socialists were involved with them. The young RSL in Liverpool had come together with the typed and duplicated Nottingham youth paper *Rally*, and *Rebel* in London and Middlesex, to form *Young Guard*, a socialist paper calling for full nationalisation, including of the banks. We got on with them and generally speaking politically were closer to them than to the IS (International Socialists) who had started *Rebel*. The very first business editor of *Young Guard* was Keith Dickinson, from Liverpool, a thoroughly nice guy.

But RSL adult documents were all their own and like nothing else from other left factions. They put forward the demand that children should be brought up in close proximity to the factory, and they followed the Louisa May Alcott tendency on billiard halls, regarding them as dens of iniquity which the Youth must be kept from entering. This was read out with disbelief. Then came the demand that the working class should have free access to libraries! 'What world are they living in — don't they know we already have free access?'

‘Huh — that just shows how often they go in libraries.’

‘It’s Ted, the lazy old bugger, he’s too idle to start from scratch, so he keeps updating his old documents,’ said Pat. He seemed to have a soft spot for Ted Grant, although he said the best of the Grantites was Jimmy Dean. But the others were quite capable of putting together amusing documents on their own, like the one that criticised the Belgian Marxist economist Ernest Mandel for having a doll which played a tune, alleging he spent his spare time winding it up and watching it dance, instead of improving his Spanish, which was terrible.

‘Do they speak Spanish well then, up there in Liverpool?’

Pat grinned back and didn’t reply. Naturally I haven’t remembered any of the serious points they made, because of this kind of stuff.

The International Group (IG) was set up in Nottingham in 1962 as a Trotskyist organisation sympathetic to the Fourth International. Most of its members were in the Labour Party. The faction in the Fourth International that Pat and Ken Coates and Peter Price were involved with was the one around Michel Pablo. Pablo was a Greek communist who had been in the mountains of Yugoslavia in the Second World War, as part of the Greek Resistance. By this time — early 1960s — he was the education minister in the Ben Bella government of Algeria. Pablo’s general idea was that you attempted to work with whoever would work with you. In the Eastern Bloc this meant working with Stalinists; in the West it entailed working with social democrats. As a guideline to action it had much to recommend it — one has to work with whoever is there. It’s a question of accepting reality as it is and building on it. The downside is that you can tend to lose sight of a wider political perspective. In later years ‘Pabloism’ became almost a dirty word on the extreme left. Pabloites were referred to as ‘liquidationists’, which sounds dire, but means the socialist/communist ideal is being gradually diluted by contact with the less pure.

Julian was always fairly scathing of Pablo, or rather, of the effect he had on others, for we never saw him in person.

‘Oh well, Pablo has uttered, Pablo says jump, so over the cliff they all go,’ or, ‘Pablo — he’s a scholar and prince, he’s above the law for mere mortals.’ Other left groups, particularly the Socialist Labour League (SLL), who loathed Pablo’s ideas on working with other people, referred to us as ‘Pabloite revisionists’ or simply ‘the Pabs’ — e.g. ‘The Pabs have got control of the Steering Committee,’ ‘The Pabs will be there,’ ‘We’re not taking insults from the Pabs.’ From its point of view, the Group considered it wasn't hooked up on theory to the exclusion of practice. A little later the word 'praxis' — meaning a wholesome and pleasing fusion of the two — became a ubiquitous decoration in every document across the left spectrum. John Baird, the MP for Wolverhampton, was 100% behind Pablo, he knew him well and apparently saw him regularly. He was in the Fourth International and often turned up to IG national meetings, cheerful and warm, but he looked ill.

* * *

'I like to wake up every morning knowing I'm in love,' Pat said sunnily. 'It makes everything worthwhile.' He shaved and opened the shop, humming and looking pleased. He was even happier when the post came and he opened a letter.

'It's from Charlie van Gelderen. He and Millie are thinking of joining us, they've had enough of the SLL. It will be something if they do, they're great comrades, they were in the Fourth International in the 1930s.'

Another couple who were in the Fourth International at that time were Sam and Doris Bernstein, they occasionally came up to Nottingham and were much prized as early members.

Another early member was Ellis Hillman, a nice little man who sometimes turned up at national IG meetings in Nottingham. He imparted a sense of fun and enthusiasm, greeted everyone affably and usually came to sit next to me, asking what had happened since last time. Pat had known him for years. As well as being in the Fourth International he was a Labour councillor in London and a member of the Flat Earth Society.

We were receiving quite a few RSL documents because Pat and Ken wanted the IG to become the British section of the Fourth International. They had had discussions in Brussels and been told that there was no chance of the United Secretariat just pulling the rug from under the current British Section, the RSL, that civilised people didn't behave like that, polite form had to be observed, Maners Makyth Man. The best way was for the two sections — the RSL and the IG — to merge. In the fullness of time some people would inevitably be displeased, but that was up to them, they could leave. But the IG would then be the official section of the Fourth International. This was Pat's dream and he followed it relentlessly. The merger saw Julian at his most grimly furious. He voted against it at every turn and vowed to walk out of the London Branch if it went ahead. Geoff Worthington too was relentlessly against it.

It took several years. The merger went ahead at Hythe Summer School 1968. We were now the IMG, the International Marxist Group, the British Section of the Fourth International.

The RSL — or Militant as it later became known, from the name of its paper — had the last laugh. They had built up a large and effective youth party at their base in Liverpool, and as many people know they gained control of Liverpool Council in the person of Derek Hatton. So they got their own back for all the sneering and negativity over their entry work. Then after such a spectacular swan song they were expelled from the Labour Party. This is what their loyalty achieved. There were no more loyal members of the Labour Party than Militant.

* * *

Some of the other left groups at this time were the IS (International Socialists) which later became the Socialist Workers Party, and the Socialist Labour League (SLL — later the Workers Revolutionary Party), and the Selbyites. These last were an obscure split-off in the 1940s from the RCP (Revolutionary Communist Party), and revolved around Harry Selby, a barber in Glasgow. Their key document was *Once More the Tactic*. The chief burden of it was on entryism into the Labour Party, which should be treated respectfully and as though it was a democratic centralist organisation, for eventually it would turn into one. A sizeable body of left opinion disagreed that this was possible. Copies of this document had been around so long you could see from the smudgy and pale letters that they had been produced in the days of the old spirit duplicators. Pat had such a machine rusting in his cellar.

Pat was always open to suggestions from the IS, although highly critical of their position on the Soviet Union — as were we all. He veered one way then another on the SLL and their leader Gerry Healy. Sometimes he would say almost affectionately 'We have some differences with those people just now, but when the barricades go up we'll all be on the same side.' But after some rancid interchange of documents he would snarl, 'They'll be with us on the barricades sure enough — those bastards will be right behind us, stabbing us in the back.'

Come May in Paris, 1968, the SLL-aligned French Trotskyists (the Lambertists) marched away from the barricades in orderly formation. They termed those who stayed 'adventurists' and 'petty-bourgeois reformists'. The rationale for this desertion was that it wasn't The Revolution, they were deceiving the masses to pretend it was, and the true revolutionary cadre needed to keep themselves intact for The 'Real' Revolution.

'That exposes them for what they are. A revolution doesn't spring up fully formed, a revolutionary situation has to be worked for,' frothed Pat, furious and jubilant at the same time.

James P. Cannon, leader of the U.S. Socialist Workers Party and of the Fourth International, wrote a document saying of the SLL: 'They stay over there on their little island where the cops don't even carry guns, and presume to lecture the rest of the world.' Of course this was true, and probably deserved. But it had a slightly negative effect on us, it seemed part of a refracted US imperialist attitude, it applied presumably to us too. So while we laughed, we were also wary of the SWP (although Pat wasn't).

The young Trotskyists we got on with the best were the IS, and the RSL. We went to joint summer camps with them, and had a good time.

There was a Trotskyist version of 'Four-and-twenty virgins' which was always sung at these camps.

Four-and-twenty Trotskyists
Went to Inverness
When the faction fight was over
There were four-and-twenty less.
Singing 'I'll split if you split
If we split at all —
We'll form the majority faction
Or don't join us at all'

Each subsequent verse was about the leader of a group — Ted Grant, Gerry Healy, Tony Cliff, Pat Jordan, Ken Coates, made up on the hoof each time, reflecting what had recently happened. They were rude about their own leaders as well as about other leaders. The IS were the most creative. As new factions formed, more verses were added. Others featured in the song were Michel Pablo, Joe Hansen, James Cannon, Ernest Mandel, John Palmer, Mike Kidron, Paul Foot, Chris Harman, the Banda brothers (usually being ludicrously violent), Jimmy Dean, Peter Taafe, John Fairhead, Juan Posadas, Harry Selby.

The Marxist youth camps were at Hythe, Sevenoaks and Kessingland and I can't remember which years they were held. Kessingland was first, I think. I went straight from work at the telephone exchange on Friday night and changed trains at Norwich Station. The stationmaster locked me into the waiting room for several hours ('You'll be safer') with a lovely big fire, and woke me up when the train came. Arriving at Ipswich, I took the milk float out to Kessingland about five o'clock in the morning. It dropped me outside the camp and I walked around the deserted chalets until I found one with a firmly closed counter, displaying the notice: 'CAMP ORGANISER — PLEASE KNOCK'. I did this, and eventually the counter flap came down and a bleary-eyed Julian peered out. I didn't know him well then.

'What the fuck's the time?'

'I don't know — I came on the milk float.' I pointed to the notice to explain my rousing him. He tore it off viciously and said, 'You'd better come in.'

'I'm perished,' I said. He put a coat on over his pyjamas and let me have his bed, then made a cup of tea.

The camp was pre-war, miles from anywhere on the east coast. The chalets and lavatory doors were splintery and mainly falling to bits, but the lavatory chains worked and the wind blew keenly from the coast which made the doors bang and kept everything fresh.

There was a big room like an aircraft hangar with an old-fashioned nickelodeon, but it played contemporary records, like Dionne Warwick. There was a French Marxist Jesuit priest who couldn't speak English but who played football on the beach, and quite a few car workers (from Coventry, I think) as well as the usual left groups. The only speaker I remember was Ken Coates. The food was awful — tinned spaghetti in tomato sauce and fish cakes for breakfast.

* * *

I think it was Sevenoaks which was owned by a married couple, Joyce and Ernie. The food was much better than Kessingland and the accommodation more comfortable, but it was a great mistake. Ernie insisted on going about the place telling terrible jokes all the time, as though we were at Butlin's. In retrospect I can feel quite sorry for him, it must be rather dampening for your best *bon mot* to be met with po-faces and, 'We don't care about that, we only care about world revolution.'

People were so incensed, it was suggested when payment was made that £5 a day be docked 'because of those awful jokes. Before breakfast too.' Julian — who had organised it — was adamant the bill had to be paid in full. 'Otherwise we'll be blackballed.'

Speakers were notably Isaac Deutscher on Trotsky ('I'm a fan of Trotsky but I don't like Trotskyists,' — saying this to a 100% Trot audience took a bit of a nerve. Fortunately, everybody laughed). Tony Cliff didn't make it from a holiday in Israel, he was detained at the border by Israeli military authorities, wanting to register his children for national service, although they were quite small and living in London. Other speakers were Robin Blackburn and Perry Anderson of *New Left Review* and the IG; Ken Coates. Ernest Mandel and Pierre Frank of the International Secretariat of the Fourth International; Leilo Basso; Ralph Miliband; Edward Thompson. I can't remember what any of them said.

Ken was in close contact with the *New Left Review* people, who had chosen the name *The Week*. We didn't see them, they were in London and they stayed with Ken when they came up. The only one I remember was Robin Blackburn, who went to IG camps sometimes. He had a lovely Chinese girlfriend, Faye, who tragically died suddenly of leukaemia. We called round at his place one time after a demo, so he and Ernest Mandel could meet and swap economic theories, I think.

'By God Robin, how much does it cost you to live here?' said Brian, in his plain blunt northern voice.

'Well, that's a good start,' Dave said irritably.

'I don't know,' Robin replied politely. 'It's my mother's place.'

His mother came in and gave us all tea and cake, which was very sporting of her as there were about a dozen of us — probably nearly half the IG membership at the time. Ernest Mandel had tea with lemon.

Mandel always looked amused, wherever he was. There was a row at the International Secretariat, Pat reported back. The RSL delegate got up to speak and mid-flow suddenly turned on Ernest. 'He's laughing at us again. Why are you doing it, you shouldn't laugh at us.'

'Then you shouldn't be so funny,' replied Ernest.

His pseudonym, used in secretariat meeting minutes, was Walter Germain, and at first Pat sometimes called him Walter. Pat's name was Peter Petersen. Ken's was Kork. Tariq's was Clarissa, just to further confuse the security services if they were keeping tabs, but it probably didn't confuse them for long. Julian picked the name Roland Kirk when he wrote for *The Week*, but Pat put Ronald Kirk and then, to be more proletarian, Ron Kirk. Brian Davey picked the name Prufrock. It was a boys' thing l think, females didn't bother.

* * *

A faction fight I remember was the one with the BLA. They were the Bureau of Latin America, and at this time they had small groups in this country. Their supporters sold the BLA paper — *Red Flag* — which was lavishly printed on expensive paper. They had very little else to do, they didn't have to contribute to it, for all the articles were written by Juan Posadas and translated from Spanish. Nor did they have to collect money to sustain it, as Posadas also masterminded bank robberies in Latin America to fund it. As I understood it — although I may be misrepresenting them — they believed in the inevitability of nuclear war, after which the peoples of the world — those that were left, that is — seeing the folly of capitalism, would then turn to socialism as the only way forward.

'Now these really are your genuine bona fide nutcases, mate,' said Pat.

Anyway, three IG members began to receive documents from them, and to take up their political position. They drafted a document which they put forward to be adopted by the IG. It stood no chance of being passed, and once voted on would lead to the expulsion of those members who had backed it. Expulsion wasn't usual for taking a different position, but in an extreme case such as this, it was inevitable.

I loathed expulsions. I still remember the sick feeling when Tricia was about to be expelled. When I first started coming over to Nottingham I had adored Tricia, and the idea of voting to expel her was horrible to me. I hoped there would be enough votes without mine, so I wouldn't need to raise my hand. In the event after the motion that Tricia and Rhoda had proposed was defeated (it was backing the Selbyite position on something or other — she was still loyal to Brian Biggins, the Scotsman who had left her) Tricia forestalled the inevitable by saying, 'Before you vote on my expulsion, comrades, I'd like to submit this.' She reached in her bag and brought out a long sealed envelope. 'My resignation in writing,' and she swept grandly from the room. Rhoda put her envelope on the table too, flashed a mocking smile at everybody, and left.

The men left around the table — Ken Tarbuck, Martin Flannery, Alex Acheson — looked from side to side at one another silently. Eventually Ken Tarbuck broke the stricken silence by saying in a reproving voice 'Well, Sylvia, you've just seen two grown women make complete fools of themselves because of men.'

'Why are you telling me?' I asked resentfully.

'So you'll learn something,' answered Ken, pointing a finger. He had been in the old RCP (Revolutionary Communist Party) that was a direct descendant of Trotsky's Fourth International, and he had all the cuttings about it. He was a mine of information on Trotskyist history. Martin said soothingly 'Oh no no, I don't believe Sylvia would ever be so foolish.'

(Years afterwards when I lived alone with lots of cats, the kitchen ceiling fell in, and with all the noise and chaos the mother-cat started giving birth prematurely. I took to my bed until I could think straight, and the cats all thumped upstairs too. The cat was in labour in a box, then she started crunching something — kch-kch-kch. She was obviously eating the kittens. Three tom-cats sitting upright on the bed looked from side to side at one another knowingly. None of them moved. It was one of the spookiest moments of my life. And it reminded me of that unspeaking moment after Tricia and Rhoda had walked out. The males were in the presence of something female and loopy, unknowable, illogical.)

Anyway, the BLA splitters were led by John Fairhead, who lived in Paddington and worked for the London County Council. The other two were Theo Melville, a museum curator who had moved to Paddington from Sheffield, and Brian Lynam, who had lived at the Bookshop, and also came from Paddington. At that time he was a bus-conductor in Nottingham and afterwards worked at British Leyland in Coventry, and led an all-out strike there which went on for weeks. Fairhead — whom I liked very much — had gone from left group to left group, and there was even at this time speculation as to whether he was some kind of police informer. In the course of time he passed into joining the really right-wing nutter organisations. But that was afterwards.

When it came to the vote to expel them I left the room. There were enough votes, they didn't need mine, although I didn't see what else they could do. But the business was draining and dreary, with an element of bizarre futility about the proceedings, for however many documents and newspapers they produced, the Bureau of Latin America did not actually have a presence in the working life of Nottingham.

John Fairhead (who was gay), I found most pleasant, he had an urbane manner and slight paunch — a somewhat stately affair which preceded him through doors and over which he held a cigarette loosely, between two relaxed and inward-facing fingers. Theo actually did look crackers, with wild eyes and hair. He had appeared quite sane when he used to come over from Sheffield with Martin Flannery.

Brian Lynam had been put in care as a baby, and Fairhead was his political mentor, which explains why he was so influenced by him. I'm sure he would never have supported the BLA normally because his roots were firmly in the industrial struggle and anyway he had too much nous. But now and again he was very vulnerable. He had walked into Paddington police station one night and confessed to them he hated society as it was constructed, he was a revolutionary and he wanted to overthrow everything. Goodness knows what the police made of all this, they probably gave him a cup of tea. Normally he was amusing company and had always pertinent remarks about the political situation. But every so often he suffered excruciating depression. One time as a teenager I got a lift to London with Sylvia and Maurice Bardiger and was to meet Jackie at a party at Brian's. When we arrived the place was in darkness.

'Now are you sure you'll be all right?' asked Sylvia, winding down the car window and looking uncertainly into the silence.

'Yes, I've been here before,' — the car disappeared into the night.

After knocking on doors in the big tenement, I was told Brian's girlfriend Jill had left him and he was very ill. A neighbour knocked at his door — he was lying on a bed in darkness, and looked dreadful, his face green with ashen shadows. He didn't look at anybody, and said, 'I'll get my coat and take you to the tube.' He came out again wearing his battered black leather jacket and pushed me forward roughly.

'I'm so sorry Brian, I didn't know. I'll be all right.'

'You can't go there on your own.' He didn't say anything else, just walked rapidly and turned corners through wild partying crowds spilling from the big Georgian houses in Westbourne Grove — strange music and black people partying in the street in a way I'd never seen before. When we arrived at the tube station he said curtly 'You'll be okay now,' and turned abruptly and left without looking at me.

I was extremely grateful to him for not just leaving me to it when he was obviously so ill. Once at the station I rang Jackie's friends Nessie and Tony Young (I knew their telephone number by heart — London VALentine 9369), and took the tube out to Ilford where they lived.

The Youngs were in the International Socialists (IS) and opposed the nuclear deterrent. Tony was the Committee of 100 lawyer. Nessie always called him Anthony. She was a staff nurse. I considered her the ultimate in sophistication. She was blonde with wild rose colouring, the very image of Summer in Botticelli's *Primavera*. She had black-stockinged knees which were much in evidence at meetings, and she wasn't fazed by anything. Brian Lynam told me he had asked her to dinner one evening and cooked his special dish, then as he was serving it up it had accidentally exploded all over her. She sat statuesquely, as though her mind was on more important matters, totally cool, wearing her dinner.

Anyway, Nessie and Tony were married for ages and lots of people went there and used their ground-floor flat in a large old house. It was covered throughout in rush matting and had big comfortable sofas and lots of cushions. They had taken Jackie under their wing, and she used their home as a base in London. Most demonstrations either started or finished at the Youngs' home in Ranelagh Gardens, Ilford, as far as I was concerned. Nessie always looked impressive, even though she often wore old clothes — she wasn't smart, which was a word and a concept I detested. ('You have nothing to worry about,' said Julian rudely.)

Eventually they had a baby, Caroline, and when I went to stay with them we walked to the shops, pushing a big old-fashioned pram through a little park. Nessie wore an old dark coat but still looked good, with her black stockings and confident manner.

* * *

Before I moved to Nottingham, for a whole winter I could think of nothing more delightful than hurrying to Tricia's little bedsit on darkening Saturday afternoons after work, walking the curve of Waterloo Crescent, and up the stairs, all the way to the top. She was recovering from a love affair. The Scottish guy she had lived with for two years had suddenly decamped back to Glasgow because he had stomach ulcers. The day he left there was a big Christmas party at the Coop, and John and Katherine brought her to it. She looked white and ill, and after the party John drove us to her old flat, scene of many parties and discussions. It was bare, with stuff in bags, waiting for her to move too. It was freezing. I made coffee and didn't ask any questions because I wasn't sure what was going on. Everybody knew Tricia would do anything for him, she was crazy about him, so why was he leaving if he was ill?

She moved into a tiny bedsit with a gas-fire and a single bed and a high marble mantel where she burned Innoxa joss-sticks. She was tall and dark, and looked good in brown, but that winter she wore a navy ski-suit. She had large, dark, rather bold eyes, and dry skin. She had trained as a ballet dancer but had grown too tall, so she became a teacher. Her movements were graceful, poised, and she always seemed to know what to do. If you were under eighteen and working at the Telephone Exchange, you didn't get paid much, and most of us worked the married ladies' shifts to make extra money. So I often worked all day Saturday and came over to Nottingham on the bus afterwards. Tricia was there with tea and I brought cakes, and we had a lovely time together, talking about the week, and she'd light a joss-stick in quiet celebration. 'Shall we have some men in, darling?' she would ask me, solicitously latching a stray lock of my hair back. I pulled a face. 'No? We won't then,' she decided, and it seemed part of winter's comfort — the fire, the friendship, not bothering with men. Later, we made a meal — cauliflower cheese or macaroni cheese usually, and the simple cooking and eating and washing up afterwards was enough.

Lots of our conversation was about politics in a wide way. She lent me Christopher Caudwell and Han Suyin. On the fireplace wall was a sketch of Nottingham streets by Paul Waplington. On Sunday afternoon there was always some kind of meeting to go to, then we'd go back for tea, and I'd leave soon afterwards, both of our weekends nearly at an end, the working week began again the next day. Waterloo Crescent was dark when I came and dark when I left.

Jobs

Nottingham was regarded as a woman's city — there was always work. If a woman lost her job she could get another one. There was work in the lace and textile industry; and jobs galore at Raleigh cycle works, Players cigarettes, the ROF (Royal Ordnance Factory), the biggest Boots in the country, Gerard soap factory (Imperial Leather), rose growers Wheatcrofts and Bardills, Ericssons engineering and various breweries. Unemployment was not a problem.

Nevertheless, after moving to Nottingham I found it difficult to get a job. Going for interviews cost money — for bus fares, hairdresser, tights, clothes — you had to look well-presented. There were times when I nearly got a job and then found the prospective employer had changed their mind, and spoke in cross tones if I rang to enquire.

Then I fell on my feet. A lady in Basford who had just started her own agency needed a switchboard operator quickly and she asked me to start straightaway. She sent me to a car firm in a cobbled space set back between Derby Road and Upper Parliament Street. I shared an office with a middle-aged man and an older white-haired lady. They were both incredibly nice and we all got on well and I heard about their families. I operated the switchboard and did sundry office duties like opening the post in the mornings and sticking the outgoing letters in the afternoons. When I told Pat he said 'Oh yes, I know him, he's CP (Communist Party).'

'I don't think so, it must be someone else. He never mentions politics but she's rather Tory and they get on.'

'I'm quite sure it's him. He has a teenage daughter, Barbara.' So he had. After that I listened to their conversations carefully but couldn't detect any political leaning from him. On Saturday mornings I had to bus to Basford to collect my wages from my employer. The second Saturday she handed over the brown envelope and said ominously, 'I'd like a word with you. I contacted the GPO in Derby and I have to tell you — if you hadn't already started work I would never have employed you. And I advise you not to mention them or you'll never ever get a job.' So that was why I'd been for so many fruitless interviews.

'Now, you've done me a favour and I'm going to do one for you. I was alarmed after speaking to Derby and rang the car firm to check how things were and they are very happy with you, so I'm fully satisfied, and you can stay.'

'Thank you very much.'

But it was going to be difficult in future. In order to get a job I needed to say I was GPO trained and that meant saying where. Miss Manderson, the Chief Supervisor, the vindictive old bitch, was making quite sure I never got a job. The GPO didn't give references but future employers would ring and speak directly to the Chief Supervisor who could say what she liked unofficially.

I stayed with the car firm for two or three months before the contract ended and they offered me the job permanently. Although I really liked the people I worked with, it was a tiny bit feudal. Being from an agency that didn't affect me, but it would if I worked there.

'Do you know who I am?' asked an unknown young man pleasantly. 'No,' I smiled back cluelessly. The lady in the office scurried over, shocked. 'This is Mr Billy,' she said. 'She's new, she didn't know,' she apologised. He was all forgiving smiles and I smiled back.

After the car firm I was sent from the agency to the NCB at Gedling, quite a bus ride out. It wasn't such a nice job, in a typing pool so huge it was more like a factory, with desks and typewriters in regimented lines. I began to regret leaving the car firm. A dose of flu terminated the job and the boredom. I worked for Brook Street Bureau for a time, liable to be sent anywhere. With agency work you didn't always have a job, but I liked the impermanence. Obviously you didn't get paid if you were sick.

I preferred to borrow money and pay it back after I got a job, rather than go to the National Assistance Board. This was at Weekday Cross, a blip in the cobbled streets of Nottingham. It was a dark and gloomy hell-hole of grizzling children and people down on their luck. Staff came round with buckets of strong disinfectant and poured it round your feet as you sat there.

A really nice job was working at Charles Butler on Meadow Lane, a clothing manufacturer near Colwick. Cognisant of the fact I couldn't be truthful and expect to get a job, I spun a web of lies that I worked for my aged father running a bookshop. Pat was contacted and played his part.

The switchboard was buttons, not plugs, but it was the same principle. I had my very own office with a dinky little stocks and shares filing cabinet, my own big desk, a brand new swivel chair specially bought and in the drawer — luxury — a big *Webster's Dictionary*.

'I've worked here for ten years,' said Christine in the next office, steaming, 'and I've never been given a new chair,' she told anybody that would listen. Boy, was she hostile. People came in and out of the office.

Sanchia, scissors hanging from her waist, was in charge of dressmaking. When visitors were coming to view stock Mr Butler would ring through and say, 'Send Janice up.' Janice was a very pretty girl who worked in the factory and who modelled the dresses for potential buyers. It was like Mr Butler not to bother with a proper model, Janice was just as good and more natural too.

Mr Butler was quite a character. 'No, I don't want to speak to that silly arse — make some excuse,' he'd say over the telephone.

'I'm sorry, he isn't here at the moment.'

Or the door would fly open and he'd breeze through with Sanchia and others dancing attendance in his wake. I liked him a lot and enjoyed working there and stayed for several months. It came to a sudden end when, attempting to reach big card file boxes on the top shelf that I never used, in order to dust them, I stood on the controversial new chair and my stiletto heel went straight through the material. Oh God. Christine was jubilant. Her refrain now was 'She's been given this new chair and look what she's done…'

The office manager was called. 'There'll be trouble about this, I'm afraid. That was an expensive chair.'

It was Friday afternoon. I said goodbye with sadness to the *Webster's* and didn't return on Monday morning. In the next January sales I took my Christmas money to Sisson & Parker's Bookshop in Wheelergate and bought a *Webster's* in its turquoise striped cover for fifty shillings.

Of all the job interviews I attended, only Charles Butler wanted to see if I could actually operate a switchboard and hear how I sounded on the telephone. When being interviewed at Raleigh I asked to see the board and work it and my request was treated as an indulgence, they weren't interested in checking how I handled calls. I find this quite extraordinary. After all I might have been hopeless but no other employer ever checked.

* * *

The Labour Exchange sent me here and there for jobs, including to the big Coop offices on Derby Road. As I waited to be interviewed Mike Sillitoe, from our Labour Party, popped his head round the door — a friendly face. 'Hello, are you coming here?'

'I don't know, the Labour Exchange sent me.'

He indicated with a finger towards a room. 'If you're going in there, he's crackers. When he interviews people he's got this machine, it records what they say. And when they've gone he plays it over and over and sits laughing to himself. He's potty, I'm telling you.' He shot back hastily behind the door, as another door opened.

The interview didn't go well. 'The only work we have,' said the Personnel Manager, 'is at the funeral parlour.'

'But that's not the job the Labour Exchange sent me for,' I objected.

'Oh, that job's gone now,' — he was manifestly lying. So I was to start the following Monday at the Coop Funeral Parlour. I wondered which bit of our conversation he would find amusing afterwards, because I couldn't laugh at any of it.

My two weeks at the funeral parlour were ghoulish in every respect. I had my own office (I would have been glad of company) and had to type out interment certificates, sometimes for people who had still been alive that morning. When I went to the loo the reception area was often full of weeping people on chairs, and I was warned not to make a noise or even offer a sympathetic smile. The male undertakers went round with po faces, even when not actually wearing their top hats. The offices were at Canning Circus, opposite the Sir John Borlase Warren pub, on its promontory between four roads, and were oak-panelled, dark and subterranean, set deep in the ground. From my desk I could see people's legs moving past outside the window. It was really gloomy. Way across two roads, through an archway into the cemetery, a memorial angel lifted its wings into the sky, ready for take-off.

It was quite busy at the Coop, because funeral costs also meant divvy. Even so, there was much spare time between typing interment certificates. As luck would have it the book I was reading was Daniel Defoe's *Journal of the Plague Year*. I'd hankered to read it for years but it was hard to come by. Raye Coggan, a Wednesday night stalwart, who came from her job at the Inland Revenue to help at the Bookshop on *The Week*, lent it to me. The story threw another gloomy cast across the day.

Often when I opened the office door came the sound of banging — the undertakers were breaking bones to fit a body into its coffin, if the person had died in an awkward position. I wouldn't have known this, if the Chief Undertaker hadn't told me. 'The last girl we had left suddenly. We find it hard to keep them.' I became scared of crossing the road in case I got knocked down and needed a coffin myself. At the end of the second week I said nothing — well, I didn't see anybody often — but knew I wasn't going back.

When I rang the Coop to try to get my wages I was told they had been confiscated in lieu of unworked notice. So I worked at a rotten job for a fortnight and didn't get paid. In fact it had cost me bus fares and fresh tights. Sod the Coop.

During jobs I fitted in work for *The Week* at the weekend, editing and putting the 'American Notes' together and cutting the stencils. Extra typing wasn't possible when I was out at work. Pat asked Rhoda to come — in between her jobs and if they were speaking — and did the rest mostly himself, although Joyce, Alan Donne's new wife, came to type sometimes. Sometimes on a Wednesday I'd go off sick from work and set-to at the Bookshop.

When at work I didn't always know what was going off at home. One time I returned to find Tricia and Tiger cleaning Pat's kitchen and throwing stuff out. They were very pleased with themselves. We hadn't seen them much since the faction fight and Tricia's resignation.

'You can't keep food for too long.' 'This is better in the dustbin.' etc. I just managed to save them from binning the chocolate spread. It was disgusting stuff but Jean was partial to it and would have been hopping mad if it had been thrown. All I wanted to do was collapse with a cup of tea. Tiger was busy piling the newly-washed plates — they hadn't been dirty — into a self-satisfied stack.

'They arrived with buckets and mops,' said Pat afterwards. 'I couldn't say no.'

'You're just a guy who can't say no,' I started singing.

Later, when we were eating tea Pat said musingly 'When Tricia was living here I was boiling over with lust for her. I was absolutely eaten up with it.'

'Oh really?' I said. 'Pass the salt, would you?'

'Yes. I was dreading her leaving but when she went I was relieved.'

Jean rolled her eyes heavenwards and didn't offer a comment.

But what was it about Pat's kitchen that brought young females to a pitch of enthusiasm for cleaning it?

* * *

I was so pissed off with the funeral parlour that I didn't get a job for a while and concentrated on *The Week* and matters at the Bookshop. In any case, whenever Pat went away — he went for two weeks a year to a Coop school in Hertfordshire and abroad now and then — I did the editing. He left me in charge.

'Does Pat nag at you to get a job?' asked Martin Turner, an immensely agreeable new member of the IG. He worked at the Gas Board and was waiting to go to Oxford.

‘Well sometimes. But not too much because he’d have to do *The Week* by himself.’

* * *

The next good job I had was at Selincourt House on Queen’s Road. It was a group of about six lace firms — Levins, E & A Richards at Ilkeston, Hicking & Pentecost, Leivers and a couple of others I can’t remember.

Once again the Labour Exchange sent me. As I was waiting to be interviewed Bob Gregory came through. ‘Have you come for a job? I expect you’ll get it — I’ll put a word in.’ This sounded promising. He was the Assistant Office Manager and in the International Group.

Valerie was the receptionist, and my job was to type in the main office and relieve her for breaks, holidays and emergencies.

‘I don’t know what her wage is, it’s different from everybody else’s, but she’s worth every penny to them, don’t you think so?’ said Bob. Yes I did think so. She was twenty-five and had worked there since the age of fifteen, and she gave Selincourt priority over everything. Nothing was too much trouble for the firm, she was always pleasant and 100% reliable. When she was twenty-one Mr Levin had given a big party for her. ‘He told me to choose a length of lace to have a dress made up.’

‘What colour did you pick?’

‘Deep red carnation.’

Upstairs, behind a big dark door we never went through, was an unknown domain shut off from our part, where the weft and warp held sway, where lace draftsmen planned their patterns and pegged them out, and twisthands spun cotton and took naps and dreamed of their weekends.

When I had occasion to go into the dark and gloomy upstairs where the bolts of lace were piled onto shelves, I looked for the carnation. It would have suited Valerie beautifully, with its figured selvedge. She was very dark, her hair kept in an expensively-cut bob.

Valerie presided over reception, which was wide and carpeted, very plush for the time, with a curved counter and plate glass windows and doors. This was unlike so many of the places I’d worked in, which only had poky little holes with a tiny window for visitors to announce themselves.

The general office was large, and I sat at a typewriter near Pat, Glenda and Christine. Pat seemed in charge but l think that was because of her personality, not because she was officially in charge. She was blonde, engaged to be married and ran a UN supporters’ branch at home. She had many enthusiasms and everybody was roped in. On your birthday you had to buy everybody a cream cake and they did the same on their birthdays. It came round quite often but was cripplingly expensive when it was your turn.

Her worst enthusiasm was the determination that Selincourt House would have its own netball team, and we were going to play in it. She managed to cadge the money for the equipment under the heading 'Sports and Social Activities'.

'I've ordered the T-shirts and they're coming soon.'

'Oh no. Pat, I do know how to play netball but I'm not any good,' I pleaded, to no avail.

We travelled on the bus in the light evening to a school on the outskirts, I can't remember where, with our new aertex shirts and navy shorts, pleated to look like skirts. It was ignominious from start to finish. The school netball team we played were aged about fourteen, much smaller than us and very skilful. Every time I turned round I knocked the little girl who was shadowing me over. We didn't get any goals. In the second half the schoolgirls kept saying sympathetically, 'Aahh, give them a chance.' It was total humiliation.

'It was all Glenda's fault,' Pat decided. It wasn't, it wasn't, we were all uniformly rotten. 'We'll have to practice before we go again,' said Pat. Oh please — no! We never did play again, thank God.

A low point at Selincourt happened when Valerie went off for her morning tea-break and I was on the board. Mrs. Lewin, Mr Levin's housekeeper, rang on the internal telephone clustered together with other 'phones on the reception counter. She was in a panic and flustered.

'Oh dear, I don't know what to do. Peter and Susan have gone to school without their lunchboxes and I can't get hold of Mr Levin, he's still on the 'phone. Can you tell him?'

'I can't interrupt the call. I'll watch it and ring him as soon as it finishes.'

When the discs flapped yellow I rang through and gave him the message. He was furious. 'You just get on with your job and never mind about Peter and Susan.' There was a horrible silence lasting about ten seconds.

Then I said, 'Mr Levin, I am getting on with my job. I'm a switchboard operator and I've just read a telephone message for you which is written on my pad. The contents of it don't interest me in the slightest.' After another horrible silence, he crashed the receiver down.

Valerie came back, and I returned to the general office. I was summoned back by her with some consternation. 'What's happened?' she asked.

I told her.

'It's not your fault,' she said loyally. 'I'll explain to Mr Levin, you mustn't worry.'

'I'm not worried,' I replied ungratefully.

When I told Bob he pooh-poohed it, waving a hand in the air. 'Don't bother about him. Yes, yes, he's the top man because he's managing director of the largest firm. But in a way, Avery is over him. He's appointed from Birmingham by the shareholders and is answerable to them. He's the one to watch. He knows his job inside out and he's good at it,' he said approvingly. Everyone was rather scared of Mr Avery. He was quick and dapper, with carefully trimmed beard and expensive suits.

I was sorry about the incident because I quite liked Mr Levin. He was large and quite plump and kindly towards the workforce. When the father-and-son owners of lace firm E & A Richards came, Mr Levin met them at Reception. As they chatted about cricket he smiled at them and nodded. Then he said, 'Football is my game,' and they both looked utterly shocked.

'Cricket, surely?'

He continued, plainly teasing them and aware of the effect he was having. 'Oh yes. I go to watch Forest every Saturday when they play at home, I'm their biggest fan...' He could say what he liked, Levins was the largest Selincourt firm. So I was sorry about the unpleasantness but didn't regret what I said, I couldn't have said any other.

'We don't want crumbs from the rich man's table, we want to take over the bakery.' I should have quoted good old Lenin at him, but it would probably have been too much for Mr Levin's delicate sensibilities.

* * *

When we went for a weekend stroll through Nottingham, Julian pointed up to the little attics near Broad Street where early lacemakers stitched their lace, they talked and stitched and hurt their eyes, candles standing against looking glasses and glass jars of water to reflect and extend the thin quivering candlelight. What became the whole Nottingham lace industry was founded on these little attics and busy working people.

* * *

Round about this time Pat said, shutting the Bookshop one Thursday, 'Come on, I'll leave Chanchal for this week, and we'll go to the pictures.' I rang into work citing a stomach bug, and off we went.

The Cartoon Cinema had opened in Market Street and it was very popular, showing cartoons British and foreign and of various periods, and it also screened old '30s and '40s and '50s films, often in glorious Technicolor. We went to see *The Solid Gold Cadillac* starring Judy Holliday — a favourite of Pat's. In the film she played a shareholder with a teeny share in a car company, which she didn't understand, but boy did she make trouble. In those days capitalism had some pretensions to be kindly, not totally cut-throat, and all was resolved peaceably, she defeated the crooked directors and it ended with a romance. At the next meeting of the IG in Pat's kitchen we discussed the film and the role of shareholders in capitalism.

* * *

Bob, as I said, was in the IG, and he and Judy lived upstairs at 54 Park Road with their big fat cat, Chairman Miaow. Bob deliberately dressed like a stage cad, in expensive suits of loud and usually brown check, often but not always with a bow tie. This was his take on work. 'You have to give a fair day's work for a fair day's pay. You have to give it everything you've got, it's a matter of self-respect, to do a good job. Just because we're socialists shouldn't be an excuse for slacking.'

He was full of energy and he often stayed late in the office to finish work. When he knew I was on the switchboard at lunchtimes he would sometimes make political calls. One I remember was a telegram to the Fourth International in Ceylon.

'Congratulations on your split from the Lanka Sama Samaja Party... Long Live the Fourth International and Workers Rights and Forward to World Revolution.'

The extra work he put in at the office more than paid for the Trot telegrams. Bob had his own viewpoint on everything. Every Christmas there was a big card on the kitchen mantelpiece: 'To Pat Jordan at the Bookshop, Season's Greetings from Jack and Pamela Dunnett' under the imprint of a portcullis. Jack Dunnett was our local MP and a big-wig at Notts County. I was at a loss. 'He sends Pat a card every year, why? He's not detectably political. And when he does vote in the Commons it's with the right-wing.'

'Oh, he doesn't care about anything but his football club,' Bob replied indulgently. 'But I expect he's acknowledging Pat as a force to be reckoned with who can make things happen. That's how he got on. He rose from poverty in the Gorbals to become a barrister and an MP. And that calls for respect, however non-political he is,' insisted Bob.

Bob often seemed to consciously play the part of a bounder. He was a leading light in Lenton Ward Labour Party and also in the Anti-Colour Bar Campaign. The main figure in this campaign was a rather grand but very nice middle-class lady called Mrs Whewell. Bob called her Sybil, which nobody else dared do.

'Oh we know you don't care about workers, especially black workers' hollered Bob at a big public meeting, to the local Tory MP Norman Fowler, who vehemently denied it.

Afterwards he came up, deeply concerned, and said 'Bob, I'd hate you to think I share that view, I'm totally opposed to racialism.'

Bob laughed jovially. 'It's all right, I know you are, but all's fair in love and war.'

* * *

On Thursday lunchtimes — or sometimes Fridays — the movers and shakers in Nottingham IG met for a Chinese in the Dragonet, and in later years the China Prince, with its famous rude waiter. Pat, Ken Coates, Peter Price, Bob Gregory were the core attenders and later Julian, Brian Simister and Tony Morris, formerly from Nottingham North YS, and then a NUPE union rep. I was asked occasionally. They discussed the ongoing struggle in the Labour Party, where the right-wing was trying to throw Ken out, and other work in general.

Joe Hansen, who had been Trotsky's young secretary when he was assassinated, paid a flying visit to Nottingham. There was no public meeting — I think he wasn't well. He met a few IG members at a restaurant round the corner from Queen's Road at lunchtime. Jean and I were overawed, but at Pat's instigation we told him of the ongoing fight to stop the Labour Party from banning our youth newspaper *Young Guard*. He said nothing, just nodded sagaciously. Afterwards he told Pat he hadn't the slightest idea what we were talking about. He probably didn't empathise, as the (US) SWP was an open Trotskyist organisation. Jean and myself had to rush back to work. Bob, being office manager, could take a more leisurely lunch break, so presumably had discussions with him at a more elevated level.

* * *

That summer I celebrated my twentieth birthday. Jean, Pat and myself went for a Chinese meal in the early evening. We were all so skint we each paid for ourselves.

I worked at Selincourt House for six months and would have happily continued there. The owners were well-off, but they were generous and pleasant to their employees. When I left at the end of the summer they put in not one week's wages owing for holiday but two weeks' wages when they sent my cards. My sister and her husband offered me a job looking after chickens while I took my GCEs. Pat advised me to go, and my IG branch voted in favour of it. So I left Nottingham temporarily.

Customers and Neighbours

When Pat started going to London I pushed the large desk in the shop that served as a counter so it stood right in front of the archway to the back. This made me feel less vulnerable. In the far corner were cowboy books ('Westerns,' insisted a shocked Romolo. 'Nobody calls them cowboy books.'). In the near corner were crime stories and in the corner next to the door were small romance booklets. This was because the readers of them — married women — were the least likely to open the door and steal. Paperback novels formed the bulk of the other books. Pat put a small bookcase out in the street, the books priced 6d each.

There were four second-hand bookshops in St Ann's and they all had a side-line. Pat's stocked political books and pamphlets. The big bookshop on Alfred Street Central sold expensive pin-up books and doubled as a brothel. 'Orange for Books', just round the corner from Alfred Street North on Mansfield Road, sold fishing tackle. One on Huntingdon Street also sold surplus Army and Navy clothes.

Dolly came in for the romances: 'Oh — I must have a read.' She lived further up the street on the same side and her four growing children came in too. Her daughter Junie, aged about nineteen, stood on the corner every night with a little gang. She was a capable young lady, small and slight, with a sheet of long blonde hair. She seemed in charge of her mother when they were together. 'Oh really — you silly woman,' she would chide. Dolly came in one time wailing that Junie had gone off with all the housekeeping money and done the shopping. 'She's come back with a lot of apples and pears, she says it will be good for us, but what shall I do? I can't feed us all week on apples and pears.' The women clucked sympathetically, the men ignored her and went right on reading their books. There was an elder son, and a clueless younger daughter, Sandra. The youngest of the family was eleven-year-old Patrick. In the middle of a nightmare he had thrown himself out of the back bedroom window on to the ground below, to the great amusement of the street, which ragged him about it. The danger involved didn't seem to trouble anyone.

* * *

Seven-year-old Janet came in sometimes for comics, but when her father, a small genial window-cleaner, fell off his ladder and broke his leg she came regularly and announced importantly 'I've come for my

Daddy's books.' He read cowboy stories (sorry — Westerns) and I was expected to remember which ones he had taken out previously. She came in one day, going through the stack of *Bunty*s while I sorted the Westerns ('The sun shone relentlessly across the mesa. The cactus flowers opened in the heat...')

Cordley arrived. 'Hello, I've come to take more photos',

'You can take a photo of me,' piped up Janet. Cordley frowned and ignored her.

'We heard there are rats round here — do you know where I can find them?'

'Cordley, why shouldn't you take her photo?'

He hedged unwillingly. This made me mad — he'd come to photograph St Ann's — why shouldn't that include Janet? She lived here, an only child, she was her mummy and daddy's pride and joy, with polished shoes and neat brown ponytail.

'Rats!' cried Janet, abandoning the *Bunty*s. 'We've got rats in our street.'

What street is that?' asked Cordley, unconvinced.

'Little John Street. Come on I'll show you.'

'Janet, you are absolutely not to show him any rats until he has taken your photo — do you hear me?'

They ignored me and went off together chatting.

* * *

Paul came to visit from the Approved School. He was such a nice little boy, mild and sweet-natured, and I couldn't imagine why he had been sent to such a place. He seemed to regard it as part of his lot and wasn't questioning of it. Whilst there some big boys had got hold of him and thrown him over a hedge and almost ripped off one of his ears, which had been sewn back on, so red bug-like scabs were in a line along the join, which I saw as he riffled through the one penny comics.

'Can't you refuse to go back there, when your ear is better?' I urged. He shrugged helplessly, mild eyes gazing through a scatter of freckles. 'No not really. They'll come and get me.'

In spite of his apparent passivity he must have had some vim, because it was Paul who had been at the directing centre of the small children seen by Jean clambering over the rooftops. Aged eleven, he obviously had hidden qualities of leadership.

* * *

Bridget came in 'I've brought our baby to show you.'

'Patricia,' I replied.

'Oh no, she's the last baby. This is Bernadette.' In the street sat the baby in its pram gurgling and smiling — another little copperknob.

* * *

Pat also ran a book service, and occasional orders came through the post, mostly for a pamphlet he published on the Nottingham race riots in 1958 — *Don't Blame the Blacks*, written by George Powe. George was a long-established comrade who was in the IG from the beginning. He had come from the West Indies in the 1940s and was, by the 1960s, a Labour councillor in Long Eaton. Orders came from Africa, and from America ('We always thought Nottingham was a mythical city associated with Robin Hood, and were surprised to learn it really exists…' — letter with order from Ann Arbor.) There were duplicated copies of pamphlets by Lenin and Trotsky.

The books read by customers weren't just romances or war stories. Favourite authors included Calder Willingham, Harold Robbins, John Steinbeck, Hank Janssen, Mickey Spillane, Sax Rohmer (*Fu Manchu*), Dennis Wheatley, Raymond Chandler, The Saint and James Bond. Many were in lurid covers, which are now highly collectable.

A night nurse came in and asked for anything by Charlotte Brontë. 'I love her but you can only get *Jane Eyre*,' which was true then. I went upstairs and found my copy of *Villette*, which as a schoolgirl had gone with me to Austria like a talisman. But the dissemination of learning was important. A lady with scads of children and even more living next door with her first husband, came in and asked for Dickens.

At one point there were twenty-one old paperbacks of *Saturday Night and Sunday Morning*, so customers must have liked to read about their own lives. My friend Chris rang from Derby Telephone Exchange to say she was coming over to Nottingham with her new boyfriend and we could meet up at the Peach Tree. I understood immediately that she had chosen that pub because it was in the book. It was in town, lit up at night with glowing orange and pink fruits. In the wake of *Saturday Night and Sunday Morning* we were in its shadow, the streets hallowed, Nottingham a magic city. We saw the film at the Savoy Cinema, where Arthur Seaton himself might have taken Brenda or Doreen. We never saw Alan Sillitoe, Ken knew him, they were involved in schemes together, but his younger brother Mike came into the Bookshop at the back.

Pat recommended I read Maxim Gorki, and I loved *Tales from Italy*. He found me an old copy of the Victorian historian John Richard Green's *History of the English People*, which he recommended as a basic. It's excellent and I still read it. My copy of Kipling's *Kim* is a paperback printed in India with '1/-' stuck on it by Pat. In its pages is a scrap of torn paper bag with Punjabi writing on. I like to think it's a spell but it's probably a shopping list. Christopher Isherwood's *Goodbye to Berlin* came in, in an interesting edition — a hardback with a photo of night-time Berlin on the cover.

David Holbrook was much read then, I borrowed library books by him. He wrote a *New Left Review* article with a heartbreaking photo of a little mill girl — so young, so vulnerable – I kept it propped up in my room. Talking of the 11+, David Holbrook said something like, 'These children are emotionally aware, for they have suffered. They know they are rejected.' It has become unfashionable now to care. Holbrook's was one of the voices in favour of abolishing the 11+. They prevailed. But the basic problem is still there.

* * *

Every three months I had to put together a box of paperback detective stories — about sixty to sixty-five — to send to Bertrand Russell. No Agatha Christies — he'd read them all — and no novels. When *Other Voices, Other Rooms* came into the shop I was lost in delight and packed that in the box too. It was a wrench but I thought Bertrand Russell would be bound to want to read it.

'There's been a complaint,' said Pat. 'Not all the books were detective stories. No, it doesn't matter if they're not well-written. He's a mathematician and he wants a problem to solve.'

He read one every night and I thought of him settling down in the evening with the book, solving the crime then going off to bed with his milk drink. He didn't buy the books, they were sent gratis because of his generosity to many different causes and all he had done. He had been a conscientious objector in the Great War, as well as opposing the nuclear bomb in the 1950s. He said all things in maths should be provable. Yet he also said that mathematics is a human dream. 'It is delightful but it is in the domain of the imagination,' like poetry, and not a knowable reality. If this is so then it's surely true also of a monetary system which is based on maths. This is a system which we can play with, and use, and change if it doesn't suit us. We considered him a precious jewel.

Pat was invited for a long weekend at Bertrand Russell's house in Wales. There was a panic on about his clothes. He always wore a suit but had no coat. His father gave him a really good dove-coloured one. And what book should he take as a gift? The back of the Bookshop was ransacked. I suggested a Victorian edition of the collected pieces written by W. H. Russell for *The Times*, sent from the Crimean War. After much deliberation and handling and pondering, Pat decided on a big old edition of Mallory's *Morte d'Arthur*, with thick uncut pages. I can't remember why. I think he had heard Russell liked King Arthur.

* * *

The Bookshop was mortgaged and in a state of utter disrepair. The slates were on the roof, but willow-herb grew behind the bath in the scullery, which held also a battered filing cabinet and an old copper for heating the water, which had then to be ladled into the bath with a saucepan.

The bank manager called at the back door, he stood there in the slummy yard in his black bowler hat amidst drifting clouds of seed from the willow-herb. 'Good morning. ls Mr Jordan in?'

'I'm sorry, he's abroad at the moment.'

'Are you his daughter?'

l smiled. 'No.'

'Oh. I see. l do beg your pardon,' — he became apologetic and gallant. 'Will you tell him I called and would like a word when he returns,' — lifting his hat politely, he went off through the rackety gate.

* * *

'Aren't you going to get rid of those weeds?' demanded Mrs Walker from next door but one. 'They're seeding in our part and we have to weed them.'

'Good,' retorted Pat. He hated his neighbours and they hated him. There was a magnificent crop of rosebay willow herb on the tiny Bookshop part, a white floss of seeds rushing upwards in the autumn winds, like a whirlwind.

The neighbourly dislike between Pat and the Walkers had its origin in the union struggle a few years before in the AEU. Both Mr Walker and Pat were members and on opposite side in an internecine bust-up. It had been a bitter struggle, which I think the right wing won, and Pat and Mr Walker were still at daggers drawn.

'He's a total shit-bag,' Pat spat venomously. Mr Walker was obnoxious in passing. We all shared a back gate and he never lost an opportunity to be snide or objectionable. He laughed in a cackling disagreeable way and made sarcastic remarks.

Dick looked down out of the kitchen window one evening and Mr Walker came through the back gate. 'Your car's parked on our front,' he shouted up.

Dick pushed the window open and responded 'So?'

'Well why don't you move it. And,' — he laughed nastily and prepared to run — 'why don't you go back to your own country?'

'What!' — Jean and myself each leapt on one of Dick's shoulders, attempting to prevent him from dashing downstairs. He tore free, but the delay was enough to give Walker time to get inside and prevent an incident.

Another time Jean and myself were eating tea and a sharp rap came on the kitchen window. It was a Walker son, with a line prop. 'It's raining on your washing,' he called up.

'How dare he?' stormed Jean.

'No, no — that's the good brother — thank you very much,' I called down.

Jean looked horrified. 'The good brother? He had the cheek to bang on our window with his prop.'

'He meant well.'

Pat was summoned and pronounced, 'That younger son does actually have a vestigial spark of human decency. Where he gets it from, God alone knows, in that household.'

The young man was always quite friendly, unlike the other three Walkers.

* * *

When Goose Fair came in the late autumn the Bookshop was deserted of customers. After closing, a few of us sauntered up Alfred Street North towards the fair. It was parked on the Forest — the biggest fair in the country. All the fairs came together before splitting up for the winter.

We wandered about in the mud and the shattering noise and push of people. The booths; ghost train; dodgems smashing and thumping; old hurdy-gurdy music which had churned out since the turn of the century; hapless plastic ducks bobbing back anyway after they had been popped; threepences and sixpences rolling down green baize to oblivion and all around people screaming and throwing their money away.

'Hello,' greeted a passing youth. 'I've seen you at Kay's.'

He meant Katherine, her family lived quite near but she scorned to go to Goose Fair.

The helter-skelter was my favourite but it cost half-a-crown. You climbed up, surveyed the fair way below and the dots of people and then whizzed down and the money was gone. It would have bought four meals. I went for the candyfloss, it was the only time you saw it unless you went to the seaside. Two fan-dancers, one small and plump and rouged, the other tall and bony, listlessly moved their feet in time to music and twitched their big fans, waiting to give a show inside a tent when enough customers turned up. 'What they should do,' piped up a cleverdick schoolboy to his friend, 'is take the fat off that one and put it on the other one.' How insufferable for the dancers to hear, but they just stared ahead and went on shuffling their feet.

Outside a booth on a raised platform waiting for challengers stood a wrestler. 'Challenge Black Jacques' said the notice. He was a thickset muscly man in a black sleeveless vest and black leotard, and with a black mask over his eyes he looked like a Tudor executioner. 'Black Jacques,' said Pat excitedly. 'That's my brother,' he claimed. Nobody believed him because he was such a liar, 'It is,' he laughed as we jeered disbelief. The wrestler — you couldn't see his expression because of the mask — stared ahead and ignored Pat, who went on laughing as we picked our way through the mud, the machinery and that whining clanking noise fairs always make.

* * *

Katherine lived near the Forest with her parents and brothers, and before moving to Nottingham I often stayed there on Saturday nights. We were both teenagers; her family had come from Cavan in Ireland when she was fourteen. Because John was a member of the International Group she sometimes came to meetings, a sympathiser rather than a member. After I moved to the Bookshop we both went to the same history evening class at Clarendon College.

On Saturday nights we'd get back late, spending the time in Katherine's low bed in the boxroom, chatting and laughing. The next day we slept until late morning, then she'd go out to check the kitchen was clear, and made us toast sandwiches with fried egg in between. We left the kitchen then to her brothers, Alex, Jim and David, who cooked the Sunday lunch, as Mrs Moran, Katherine's mother, went to midday mass on Sundays. We all sat round the kitchen table to eat, minus the parents.

On weekday evenings Mrs Moran was at work. She was a night nurse at Mapperley Hospital, and good-natured Mr Moran presided while a succession of young people from the area knocked at the front door and then walked straight in. From the boys' bedroom usually came the sound of Billy Fury ('Halfway to Paradise') while Alex, Katherine's twin, did gymnastics and larked about with his great friend Michael. I thought the free and easy ways of so many young people was great but Katherine pulled a face. 'It's like living in a railway station.'

One night we went back with John, and went to bed leaving him talking to her brothers and various young visitors. The boys cooked up a plan to put recording equipment in Katherine's room to find out what the girls talked about. John was adamantly against.

'I must protest. It's a gross invasion of the girls' privacy.' But he was ignored. He was alarmed in case we might be speaking of his relationship with Katherine, they were on occasion sleeping together and he was anxious we would mention it and her father would hear, as he sat in the corner reading his paper and enjoying the young folks all around.

Meanwhile, in the bedroom we were in the middle of a chat when a smiling Alex knocked on the door and asked to borrow a plug because one had fused in their bedroom. He surreptitiously plugged in the recorder. When the tape was played to all and sundry we were talking about Mr Gladstone and Lord Palmerston, and Home Rule. A terrible squeaky voice trilled 'Oh but I absolutely love Mr Gladstone.' The boys were shocked but not in the way they had anticipated. Mr Gladstone was very popular with Katherine too. In later years I heard him on the radio — nobody believes this but it's true — and was transfixed. In a compelling deep bass baritone he said, 'This is a device of Mr Marconi.'

John needn't have worried, we wouldn't have been discussing their relationship. We never talked of it. But she might have been talking of her parents. Katherine was remarkably detached about them and could easily have been saying 'As soon as she met him she meant having him, she didn't care he was a Protestant, she thought she could fix it. She's like that, she thinks she can fix anything. He fell for her too but he wouldn't have done anything about it, he's too easy-going, he left it all to her. She sorted it out with the priest, and both families.'

This would hardly have gone down well with her father.

* * *

'Kathy, I'd like a word.'

'What is it, Pat, you old rascal?'

'Could you give a little talk on Ireland — the political parties and what they stand for. It need only be about four minutes in the Bookshop kitchen. Our younger members don't know much about it.' Kathy looked like the cat that got the cream, she was more than capable of doing it.

* * *

Sometimes the shop made so little money I had to adjust my diet. Sausage meat was 8d for half a pound, and fried with onion it made three meals. Risotto with rice, onion and an oxo cube was very filling, as was hot potato salad — chopped potatoes casseroled in vinegar, with bacon, mustard, onion and lots of sugar.

When Julian came he made curry and took off to a local shop to get the ingredients — tiny amounts of fresh spices and herbs, weighed out and put in paper bags. He had to run the gauntlet of ribald remarks from Indian lady customers. 'If you can cook you can come and live with me,' said one, and the others tee-heed and swayed with mirth.

* * *

Over the allotments an autumnal mist drifted as Alfonso made towards his plot, with its turned-up soil and tree against the fence. He cast a practised eye over the tree, a hawthorn, then felt the tape bound round its bough. In the spring he had taken a knife and made a cunning slit and then pushed in a stick of pear branch, taping it securely. It came from his foreman at Hicking & Pentecost, in exchange for a small flask of Neapolitan liqueur and a promise of future pears. His fingers now moved experimentally on the tape, checking it was secure and the branch still alive. He had learned how to graft fruit from his grandfather in Montella.

The old apple tree in his patch of garden in Festus Street now brought forth not only fat cookers that had dropped from the tree for years but four other types of apple... There was no more room in the tiny space behind the house, so he had grafted the other varieties onto the tree. Eventually, unable to believe his good luck and how easy it was to acquire an allotment, he had taken this one at Hungerhill, a ten minute walk from his home.

* * *

When Romolo's family first came from Italy they sat in the dark at nights, tuning to stations on the wireless to pick up strains of Bandiera Rossa and watching the flickering firelight.

Avanti popolo, alla riscossa
Bandiera rossa, bandiera rossa
Avanti popolo, alla riscossa
Bandiera rossa trionferà.

In the cold winter mornings Romolo and his brother Joe dressed hurriedly. Their parents had left early to start work. Elena in a hosiery firm, Jersey Kapwood, and Salvatore at Beeston Boilers. There was no fire and they got their own breakfast — cornflakes shuffled hastily into a bowl with cold milk. Then aged nine he fell on his feet. He had defended a boy at school, Michael Wood, who was always picked on by other boys. The next morning on his way to school he was hailed by Michael Wood's mother, who invited him in. The father was there too and he gave him half a crown (Half a crown!).

'Could you look after our Mikey please? We think you can help him,' he said. Then the mother pressed a breakfast on him. The table was laden with food, just like a picture in the *Beano* — hot sausages — he thought of them sizzling into the air in wavy lines, bacon, mushrooms, baked beans. Then hot buttered toast with marmalade. Afterwards he felt quite guilty about Joe who, like himself, had had cornflakes and cold toast.

After that he walked Michael to school every day and the breakfasts were a regular treat for two years, until senior school parted them and the icy mornings were back again.

'Now winter is here, come to the warm Dane Street Bookshop and read all the books and comics you like...' — a drawing of a little man with a big smile sitting in an armchair, a pile of books nearby. Outside the window snow was falling in fat white spots but inside was a great big comic-book fire. He had put the leaflet in his pocket and decided to go there.

* * *

The Bookshop backdoor stood across from the backdoor of the Misses Best, two sisters who had grown up there as children and then grown old. They were not very agreeable, although Annie, the younger, could be pleasant. Pat had no time for them at all, there had been a constant petty niggling over too many years. The blue brick yard still had a white line where, a few years' before, Rhoda, fed up with bickerings about her little girls going onto the Bests' part, had taken tape measure, paint pot and brush to draw the line over which the small Tarbuck girls weren't to cross.

Every so often there was a big row and the Bests rang Pat's mother to complain. His neighbours brought out the worst in him. There were times when he seemed like a naughty child. Any cooking experiments of his that went wrong, he sneaked out at night and emptied on the Bests' back doorstep. Another time Bob and John had come through the back gate and then gone right up to the sisters' window and pulled faces at them. 'They migraced at us through our own window' they reported to Mrs Jordan. Once again Brian was deputed to go round and smooth things over. He knocked at their door and announced, 'Hello, I'm an off-duty policeman. I hear there's some trouble with next door.'

The old ladies fell on him and dragged him inside, pouring out their complaints.

'Oh, I am sorry, he must be a very difficult neighbour, I'll do what I can,' Brian said. He stayed quite a long time and when he got back he told us what had been said.

'I meant every word, Pat. Those poor old ladies, I wouldn't want to live next door to you.'

Pat, suitably chastised, grinned and took the criticism with good grace. Then he said mildly 'You haven't had years of their pettiness.'

So things quietened down with them for a while. Miss Annie Best spoke to me if she had a complaint, Brian arranged it, as I'd always been polite to them. Although she was slightly more approachable, even she could be gratuitously nasty. One day two small boys, aged three and four, came up from the back gate, like a little bit of pale magic. I went downstairs to speak to them. They had light ginger hair and stood clinging to one another, uncannily similar but slightly different sizes. They weren't doing anything wrong and were terribly shy.

'Hello — what are your names?'

They blinked and clung harder to each other, their little heads inclining as one and then whispered, 'Anthony Peter Kearney — I'm four,' and, 'Andrew Michael Kearney — I'm three.' These had to be Bridget's little brothers.

A door cracked behind them. Miss Annie Best came out and snapped 'Clear off. Get on your own part.'

‘They’re only babies,’ I protested.

She began walking slowly towards them. ‘Go on. Clear off.’ As she came nearer they silently turned and left.

‘Do you have two little brothers?’ I asked Bridget when she came in.

‘Yes. Anthony and Andrew. They’re the only boys we’ve got.’ The boys in that family were obviously not as stroppy as the girls. They never came in the yard again.

Several years later when St Ann’s had been condemned and was waiting to be pulled down I was living with Julian and went back to the Bookshop every day so heard the news. Apparently, a bunch of small boys had broken into an electricity sub-station. ‘KEEP OUT’. One of them, aged nine, fell immediately, dead. The other children, including his younger brother, all left and went somewhere else to play. When the dead child was found the police went round St Ann’s streets with a loudspeaker on a van late at night, calling for his brother to come home. The brothers were the two little boys who had come into the yard. (This must have been the one accidental death in the statistics in Ken Coates’s book.)

* * *

Pat often went to his parents for Sunday lunch and he sometimes asked me, particularly if he suspected they were going to tell him off, on the assumption their remarks would be muted with me there.

They had a lovely council flat in Morley Court. Mr Jordan worked as an electrical engineer at Ericsson Telephones. For years he had been a GPO telephone engineer with his brother. They travelled about the country together with their families, mending and installing telephone wires. Their wives were sisters so the families were close, especially as they hadn’t stayed in any one place for long. Pat was born in Peabody Buildings, London.

Mr Jordan was strong Labour and mostly supported Pat, but sometimes he could be irritated by him too. Both his parents seemed to veer uncertainly between being proud and then ashamed of him.

Pat’s mother was a fantastic cook, although her poor hands were swollen and riddled with arthritis. She seemed elderly but still had amazing violet-blue eyes. She quizzed me about the Misses Best next door, but understood they could be difficult as she had worked at the Bookshop at one time and knew them.

Their son Peter was quite a bit younger than Pat. ‘Look at these muscles, Sylvia. How about that?’ said Mrs Jordan, proudly showing a photo of him flexing his biceps. 'He's a wrestler in his spare time to make extra money, as he's training to be a doctor.'

'He was at Goose Fair when we went,' said Pat, shooting me a triumphant look across the table.

* * *

'What a beautiful baby,' I said to a customer, who had left her child sitting up in its pram in the street. It was quite safe to do this then. 'What do you call her?'

'Anne. My psychiatrist is responsible for her. "You'd feel a lot better," he said, "if you had a baby." My husband played fucking merry hell when I told him. "It's all right for him, he doesn't have to keep them," because he's got children with his first wife.' The baby was so lovely and beautifully dressed, she seemed nothing to do with the little rather shabby woman who came in to buy romances.

* * *

Jean never mentioned her psychiatrist, she didn't vouchsafe details of their exchanges, except to say he'd arranged for her to have a year off. I hardly ever saw my psychiatrist, but the social worker, Mrs Tate, came to the Bookshop regularly, every two months. She was a psychiatric social worker with a degree from Belfast University. She was small, blonde and Irish and we got on well. We talked about the past but also about books and cats.

'Will you be terribly disappointed if there isn't a revolution?' she asked.

'Oh but there will be. There has to be. There's so much unfairness, don't you think?'

She was non-committal. 'We'll have to see.' Mrs Tate came from a large family, and she had five children herself. I sometimes asked about them and about her other patients. She was non-committal about them too, but once she broke out, 'Oh, I get sick of them sometimes. Whatever happens it's always somebody else's fault, even if it's the milk pan boiling over. They don't take any responsibility. That's the difference, you know, between those who grow older and those who grow up. You must always take responsibility for your actions.'

I looked forward to her coming, for we talked of many things. She had been coming for about two years when she saw my latest library book *The Allegory of Love* by C. S. Lewis. 'It's a lovely book, isn't it, are you enjoying it?'

'Oh yes. I've read another of his books too, *The Five Loves*. Agape is absolutely the best, isn't it? Eros is just a troublemaker really.'

She looked uncertain and replied, 'We-e-ell, they all have their place.' Then she said 'He was my uncle, you know. It's so sad. We didn't like him, every year a great groan went up round the breakfast table when the letter arrived saying he was coming. We had to be on our best behaviour and it was our summer holiday, we wanted to run round and shout and enjoy ourselves. And he never spoke to us. Mealtimes were silent. It's desperately sad. I realise now he had that sympathy with children — his books show it. But it wasn't expressed in life. I love his books now, and my children have been brought up on them and they love them too. So I've tried to make up to him for it in that way. But he'll never know,' she said sadly.

* * *

Another customer who had had a psychiatrist was Harry. He was one of my favourite customers. He was expansive and affable, and he seemed to know everybody. You wouldn't guess he'd had what he called 'nervous trouble'. He'd had difficulty holding down jobs until he became a window cleaner, which he liked because he was his own boss and wasn't confined inside. He had grown-up children and a young wife with small children. 'The doctor says to me, "Your wife has enough children to cope with," and I says to him "Well you know how it is, doctor, you love your wife..." and he says "Yes but she's only twenty and she's had four children. It's time she had birth control." I says to him "Dr O'Brien, when I see Father Flanagan I'm going to tell him what you said." Well. He blenched. He went white, he did. I was only ragging but he didn't want to cross the priest.'

Harry chuckled away. It was obviously a well-honed pub story, and the doctor's observation wasn't the point of it. They lived in a two-up, two-down house, with a rent of 16/- a week.

'That isn't much.'

'No and you don't get much, neither,' he replied. 'There's bowls and buckets in the bedrooms, to catch the rain. It's been like it for months...' he said energetically. Whatever happened, he never seemed down or deflated, he wore nice warm clothes — a big overcoat — and he always looked clean, with a friendly word for everyone. If I wanted to know anything about St, Ann's I asked him. He sometimes asked after Pat, but never by name. 'How is he?' He'd jerk his head towards the back. Or

'What's he up to now?'

'He's in Addis Ababa.'

'Addis you what? — where the bloody hell's that?'

'Ethiopia.'

'Ohhhh — half a minute, I know — that's old Ali Selassie, him with a beard. So that's where he is. The Lion of Judah,' he pronounced slowly, experimentally. 'Has he met him then?'

'I don't know. I shouldn't think so.'

(Several years later I was walking up Mansfield Road and who should be walking down but Harry. St Ann's was demolished and we hailed one another enthusiastically. He looked fine but shook his head. 'I've had a heart attack and when I came out of hospital I found my wife had put the kids in care and run off. I've lost everything. Everything.' I felt so sorry for him. But she perhaps had felt trapped since she was a young girl.)

* * *

Pat was always sympathetic to women. 'Females have a rotten deal in this society. If there's anything I can do to help, I will.'

One early evening Jean and I were getting ready to go to the YS. Pat had a little smile on his face and was tidying the kitchen with more care than usual. 'Don't rush back. I have a visitor coming.' Jean and I looked at one another. In fact he'd worn a little smile all day.

Off we went to take on Fishface ('I'll stick up for you but the Party won't like this resolution…'). When we returned we sniffed the air suspiciously. There were pale ale bottles on the small table and two glasses, one with lipstick on, and Pat looking pleased with himself. 'Did you have a pleasant evening? Who was your visitor?'

'Oh, it's nobody you know,' he said airily.

'He had a letter today and he didn't mention it. He put it straight in his jacket pocket.' We talked about how to get it. Of course, it was nothing to do with us, but we wanted to know. Jean asked Dick to ring very late, when Pat was in bed and in his pyjamas, and keep him talking. She called 'Pat, Dick wants to speak to you urgently,' and banged on his bedroom door. He came, blinking and fumbling with his spectacles and wrapping round his dressing gown, and took off downstairs. His jacket was on the chair in his room. We went hurriedly through the pockets and brought out an envelope. The short letter went something like:

Dear Pat, thank you for helping me, your (sic) the only person l can turn to. I'll come on Wednesday when your alone. I don't want to upset the girls. Thank you again for your help, its good of you.

It was signed with an initial not a name, but l can't remember which one.

'Why would it upset us?'

'She may be repeating one of Pat's own expressions — "l don't want the girls upset."'

We giggled at the idea, as though we were delicate little violets.

We hurriedly put it back and made coffee and Pat finally came upstairs. 'Sometimes l wonder about people,' he said, shaking his head. 'You think you know somebody. Dick's been in the movement now for years and he knows about handling union meetings and yet he needs my advice about some simple little thing that's going to crop up. He went on and on. It's really getting to him, he sounded obsessive.' We stared intently at him and nodded and Jean gave him the coffee.

No explanation of the note or the visitor was forthcoming and there were no more lipsticked glasses. Whatever it was, Pat never breathed a word.

This may be nothing to do with it, but several months later a letter came for Mrs Ann Something from the VD clinic, reminding her she had failed to keep an appointment. Nobody had heard of her. Pat shook his head, apparently mystified when shown the letter. It's possible he had offered to help her by suggesting the Bookshop as a postal address. Domestic violence was rife round there, she may have had a husband who would have turned nasty if she'd told him.

* * *

When Pat said Dick had been in the movement for years it was true. Nothing demonstrated it better than Dick's words when Pat announced veteran Trotskyist Bob Pennington was coming up from London.

'Ah, Bob Pennington. I have been in a great many cold rooms with Bob Pennington.' said Dick. Meeting rooms usually were cold, and Dick seemed to feel it specially, he was often hunched up, shivering and sniffling. Dick's wife was religious and often at church, which he found trying. 'I've told them — my work puts the food on the table and if there's any praying round here you can pray to me.'

'That's a terrible thing to tell children — it gives them no let-up from your authority.'

He laughed. 'No, and that's how I like it.'

* * *

'Kennedy's been shot,' announced Pat, appearing in the doorway when I was on the telephone to Dave about YS business. 'Don't tell lies — oh it's Pat, lying again,' I explained to Dave, but Pat was nodding his head vigorously. The telephone was in the Bookshop and had a coinbox attached, so Pat wouldn't be landed as in the past with a monster bill.

The customers used it too, so there was a stream of people in and out, to ring up for jobs or make dental appointments. Susan from round the corner on Alfred Street Central came in now and then to use the telephone, and it was a major dramatic production.

'Hello? Hello — Hicking & Pentecost? Can I speak to Andrea Smith please?' — she included all the customers in her smile and informed them 'They're putting me through.'

'Hello — are you Andrea? You don't know me, my name's Susan and I'm Vincenzo's girlfriend.' She paused meaningfully, to let this sink in. 'Oh? Oh? Well I heard he's going out with you. He isn't? No? Well I thought you might not know about me so I thought I'd give you a ring. We've been going out for some time... the thing is,' — she lowered her voice confidentially but so we could all hear — 'the thing is, I'm very jealous, I have a very passionate nature...' The women in the shop exchanged big grins; the men shifted uneasily and peered more closely at their books.

'I can't help it, that's how I am... Yes. Oh yes. Will you? Oh thank you.' Susan was obviously getting on with this Andrea. Eventually she put the receiver down and announced triumphantly to the entire shop 'She says she's going to keep her eye on him, and if she sees him with anyone else she's going to let me know.'

* * *

One Saturday morning a schoolboy parked his bike outside the Bookshop and came in and announced 'I've come from West Bridgford to play chess with Romolo.' After that he came most Saturdays.

Another customer who liked to play chess was Harry Croft. He would call in on his way home from work dressed in his gasman's uniform, and wait his turn for a game. Harry dealt in second-hand books, so usually had a rucksack of them to offer Pat, and they would stand there discussing them, intent and earnest. He had an open, rather weather-beaten face, with small, round, innocent brown eyes, which blinked a lot behind round spectacles. He looked like a friendly bear. He wasn't in the IG, but was sympathetic to the left generally. I think he may have been in the Communist Party. He liked to keep abreast of what was going on and loved to chat about political tendencies and was upfront with the latest gossip and expressions. Of Nottingham Communist Party he said: 'Oh they're very ltalianate there, you know.' This didn't mean they were sharp dressers, it meant they were soppy communists like Togliatti.

He loved to sit and watch the Bookshop children at their game of chess, perhaps it was part of a workerist fantasy he nurtured. He was a generous man and often brought books that people needed. Pat must have told him I was taking English Literature because after that each sack he brought somehow always included books needed for the course, including a lovely pencil-annotated Chaucer, with gilt pages and marbled paper ends inside leather covers. He had that inclination to help which is impersonal and part of a general impetus to good. The Van Loon sketch of himself and a friend like specks in a snowbound world, entitled *Standing there like Immanuel Kant with the starry heaven above us and the categorical imperative in our hearts*, makes me think of Harry and those like him in that world of Nottingham in the 1960s.

Periodically he was thick with Rhoda. I don't think they were political allies, except in the most general left-wing sense. Rhoda got involved with the BLA which undermined her credibility on the left for some time, and she and Harry cooled off, although I don't think they fell out.

Voices

'Look at them standing on the corner there — them Italian men are cheeky-daft,' said Dolly, peering between the Vietnam posters on the glass of the Bookshop door.

*

'Wild Thing,' hollered Bridget, waving her arms about as though semaphoring; thrusting one hip and then the other, giving the customers her rendition of the current Troggs hit. 'You make my heart sing...'

*

'There goes Rosa,' said Dolly, as a small woman hurried past the window. 'She's going back to Italy next year. I wish I'd got somewhere sunny to go back to,' she said wistfully. Everybody called her Dolly, but when we were in the Freeman's Arms there was a raffle and customers wrote their names on the tickets. 'DOLL' she printed slowly, in big square capitals.

*

'Alec, if you leave your school exercise book here again I shall put it in the one penny comic pile and sell it.' Alec, a cheerful West Indian boy, who did his homework in the Bookshop, rocked with laughter. 'You can an' all, and good riddance.'

*

'One of the cruellest things you can do is to whip workers with the knout of false optimism.' Oh no — that wasn't a Bookshop voice, it was Trotsky on the shelves in the back.

*

'Ange,' whined the little kid. 'Go on. Aw, go on, Ange. Angelo. Let me. Let me, Ange, Go on.'

'Shuddup,' said Ange, not lifting his eyes from the pages of *Nick Fury, Agent Perilous*, a finger poised, mesmerised, ready to turn the page.

Summer in St Ann's

When the rain came windows were wide open to it, moisture seeped through the streets, refreshing the air. I loved the summer rain and sat by the window with a mug of coffee listening to it sing in gutters and hit pavements like spilling beads

The Bookshop stood at the end of Dane Street in a row of houses, with an extra floor more, so it stood tall and thin in a terraced line. Dane Street was known as Italian Street. The children came into the Bookshop — the boys, anyway. The Italians appeared not to have girls, they were never seen on the street. In the mornings they were hurried into cars and driven off to Catholic school — giving us a quick glimpse of much-ringleted hair and big dark eyes, like dolls with souls.

One day Jean and I were taking in shopping from the milkman's van when a junior girl broke away from a car and rushed up. 'I like you,' she said with a big smile. I smiled back before a great scream came down the street — 'Marrrrrreeeea,' — putting more emphasis in the name than an English voice can ever do, and the little girl darted back.

* * *

Pat said when the Italian ladies had babies a big satin bow was hung above their front door — white satin for a boy, blue for a girl. 'Blue for a girl?' I echoed.

'Blue is the Virgin's colour,' he explained, smiling. 'White is for purity.'

One day a big pink satin bow went up. 'Well those are the first pink ribbons we've had in the street,' said Pat. 'They must have been here quite a while.'

I asked Romolo about blue for a girl, white for a boy. 'Never heard of it.' Then, slowly, considering 'It might be the custom in some local place. It definitely isn't pink for a girl — there's no word for pink in Italian anyway. Although,' — he shook his head — 'it could be pink for a girl by now. From outside. America?'

* * *

On summer Sunday mornings the Italian men were out in the street, polishing their cars and listening to full-throated Mario Lanza. 'Be my love, for no one else can end this yearning...'

In the summer school holiday the children were all over St Ann's streets and yards, up to all sorts. A knot of them were clustered about a tree in a backyard on the other side of the alley. More children arrived as a fire-engine hurtled through the streets, its bells clanging. Paul was halfway up the tree, a tiny black kitten looking down on him from way above and meowling. Surinder, eight years old, her toddler brother on her hip, stood watching, Bridget and Teresa dancing around the big men in their shiny helmets who descended from the fire-engine. More children began to clamber over the engine and poke the equipment. With a noisy whoosh the ladder was pulled out. One of the firemen leapt up the ladder, reached out and unceremoniously picked up the howling kitten by the scruff of its neck and came down, to ear-splitting cheers from an admiring audience.

There was a grandeur about it we have lost now — the might of the state at the pull of these little raggedy children and their kitten, as though declaring, 'These are slums and this is just a kitten, but they are our slums and the kitten matters.' No expense was spared. In later years when the small-minded penny-pinching started it didn't save money, because human locusts descended and worked out ways to make themselves ridiculous sums of money at the expense of society.

* * *

In the summer holidays Chris Holmes arrived with his suitcase on the train from Cambridge, where he was reading English. His family lived in a big house in Nottingham, they weren't working-class and although he visited them sometimes he stayed at the Bookshop for the duration. Katherine and I were pleased to see him, but for some reason his presence could agitate Pat to a pitch of irritation. 'Of all the useless clueless gormless shiftless…' he spluttered. 'That potato putting out feelers down there on the shelf has got more about it than Chris Gnomes. I respect that potato.' All eyes in the kitchen swerved towards the lauded potato bursting with seeds. 'It's attempting to fulfil its task. It isn't in the earth, it gets no food or water, conditions are not favourable to it,' he held up a stern chiding finger, 'yet it is trying its best to perform its mission in life. Gnomes just sits there like a lump, letting me trip over his bloody legs to get to the kettle — he doesn't even offer to make a cup of tea…'

'Well you'll have to tell him. He needs direction. Tell him to make a cup of tea or staple *The Week*, and he'll do it.'

Chris set to work with a will on Wednesdays, helping out. And he did actually once make a cup of tea. It was excruciating to watch, as he ponderously untied the pom-pommed tassels on the tea cosy knitted by Pat's mother, explored the way they were held together, then pulled open the cosy top and slowly lifted the teapot lid out. Oh my God.

Julian got on with Chris but they always spatted as well because Chris was a Leavisite, or at any rate a sympathiser.

'He's right, don't you think, that literary criticism should be involved with society and how it works?'

'Well, I think he's more interested in an intellectual elite,' responded Julian.

'But they're not elitist. His wife is fantastically nice, she took a group of us to the pictures and treated us to tea and cakes afterwards.'

* * *

An IG meeting in the Bookshop kitchen I remember — there was a group of YS members and Pat. Chris sat in the armchair nearest the door and Dave came late. 'Ah Holmes, you've arrived,' he said affably. 'Ablitt,' responded Chris cautiously.

'We were just discussing our attitude to the impending proscription of *Young Guard*,' said John. 'And we were exploring if there is anything we can do during the summer, before the Labour Party executive meets again.'

Dave nodded. Then he picked up a big canister of talcum powder that was standing on a table, toyed with the opening, and experimentally gave a large chug with it above Chris. A heap of powder landed on top of Chris's head. He sat, still, phlegmatic, while everyone looked dazed, even Dave. After about half a minute Chris leapt to his feet and grabbed Dave by the collar and attempted to seize the powder. They grappled together over the canister, and Chris reached into a corner and sprayed aerosol while Dave shot powder everywhere in the tangle, and tried to reach the butter on the table. Pat put it out of harm's way.

'Hide the flour and the chocolate spread,' I said to Jean, who was sitting near the food shelves, as the pair rolled round on the floor casting powder everywhere. Pat grinned and looked patient, as vegetables spilled out and crockery shuddered and we moved our feet as they came tumbling by. Suddenly they split, both of them smacking at their sleeves and trousers, sending out white clouds. Chris got up and went to sit in the armchair, wearing an untroubled expression. Dave went to lodge on the high stool. Neither seemed bothered about the ruckus or the scatter of talcum powder or the vegetables rolling round the floor.

‘Look at you,’ said Chris conversationally. ‘You look like Satan incarnate.’ Dave, it has to be said, did rather, with dark springing hair and saturnine black brows, and grinning at the description.

‘Does anybody want to pursue this about *Young Guard*?’ enquired John.

Footsteps on the stairs, the door flew open and Katherine was there in her Sunday best. ‘Is your meeting over? John and I are going to the pictures. Heavens — whatever have you been doing?’ she enquired, surveying the snow of powder over everything.

* * *

Jean’s parents called on their way to the Lake District and generously took us both to a steak house. They were sailing people from Banstead. Her mother especially was bewildered by Jean’s politics and by St Ann’s, but she tried with a pained look to understand. ‘There are some very nice Americans, you know, dear,’ she said reprovingly when we spoke of Vietnam protests. Jean gave a big exasperated sigh.

* * *

In a house on Festus Street Alfonso was packing his cases, preparing to visit his relations in the outlying area near Naples. He went back most years with his wife and small son. He glared at his wife’s cases. She had more luggage than him. Just like a woman. He suspected her of sleeping with his best friend. He was going to catch them out one day, when he had time. Perhaps when they got back from holiday. He had women, but it was different for a man, everybody knew that. He had an Anna in Stoke on Trent and an Anna in The Park and others as well.

He smiled as he remembered this time last year. He had driven his neighbour Steve to the airport. Steve was going back to Nigeria to visit his large family, and he wore full Nigerian robes. Alfonso walked behind him carrying his suitcases, while he strode ahead. They boarded the plane, Alfonso addressing him loudly as ‘Master’. ‘Yes Master, No Master. Are you comfortable, Master?’ Steve didn’t reply, as befitted the status of a Nigerian Chief. Chief for a day.

Afterwards, in the winter, the pair of them enjoyed reminiscing about their piece of homemade theatre in the snug of the Westminster Pub.

* * *

In the cobbled court behind Westville Street the Wingate brothers gave exhibitions of gymnastics in the summer holidays. There were four or five of them, their father had been in the Merchant Navy and had acquired tattoos and a skill with acrobatics, which he taught his sons. They did handstands, rolls in the air and juggled balls and as a finale climbed on top of one another to form a swaying tower of boys, while the little one did accompanying handstands. All the kids in the court clapped and Elena came out with a big steaming plate of fragrant spaghetti and butter to give them.

* * *

In July there was a party at 54 Park Road to celebrate the Cuban Revolution. At the Bookshop we were duplicating a leaflet to take, the back was full of people who spilled over into the shop, and they let in customers who knocked at the door. About 9.30pm the telephone rang. 'Tell 'em we're on our way,' I shouted through.

'No — they've rung to say don't come, the floor's fallen in.'

At work on Monday Bob turned up with a big grin. 'So many people came we all went through the floor.'

* * *

Chris and John were founder members of the IG and Chris obviously identified with it rather than with his family. He and Dave seemed to make a bee-line for one onother in order to scrap. 'I see you have an instinctive rapport with the working class,' remarked Chris sarcastically, after Dave had exchanged rancorous words with one of the ode ladies wi' fruit in their 'ats.

Pat actually wasn't hostile to Chris, he was tolerant of his presence for a couple of months.

* * *

Frank Bartlett, of Clifton College, rang to ask where he could get 'two donkeys for Thursday.'

'Christ knows what for. I suggested he ring John Daniels. If the worst comes to the worst we can push Holmes and Ablitt into a pantomime horse costume and send them,' Pat said.

* * *

The impending proscription by the Labour Party of *Young Guard* was ongoing and we decided (after the talcum powder meeting) to have a public meeting in Slab Square. We joined up with the local youth SLL, whose paper *Keep Left* was also for the imminent chop. Why this would interest the general public, goodness knew, but we gave out the leaflets anyway.

Pat Straw, from *Keep Left*, got up to speak. She was a teenager — we were the same age — and I was impressed by how she was able to cope with anything. This was put severely to the test when Yates's Wine Lodge decanted Scotch Joc and his mates into the Square.

'Now then, Mary, what are ye saying?' called Joc.

'Yes, that's my second name,' answered Pat pertly, unintimidated by his aggression and drunkenness.

'Look, ye're not making sense — are ye for the Labour or against?' he insisted.

'Yes we are,' she contradicted. 'We're for Labour. But we don't think it's fair they're closing down our newspapers... We want you all to support these two papers, *Keep Left* and *Young Guard*...'

'Give the lass a big hand, give her a big hand,' Joc chivvied his mates.

I'm not sure anybody in the Square was any the wiser, or had they been, what they could have done about it.

*Keep Left*ers were in Nottingham North YS. I didn't see them, although sometimes I crossed Peas Hill Road to put leaflets through to a little nest of them in Caroline Street. I rapped at the door and shoved the leaflets through and they acknowledged with a wave from the upstairs jutting window.

Although decrepit, the houses there were passaged and quite big. The street was named after the recalcitrant queen of George IV, and Alma Revill, the screenwriter and wife of Alfred Hitchcock, was born there.

I associate the expression 'cheek by jowl' with the eighteenth century, which still had a presence in St Ann's. People sat out in the streets on doorsteps, entries led to tiny cobbled courts with other arrangements of houses.

In summer, winter coats and blankets were pawned. There was a big pawnbrokers on St Ann's Well Road, like an outpost of a different era. Shirts with collar studs, looking as though they'd hung there since Queen Victoria's day. Cooking pans, clocks and watches piled together. Cheap and surprisingly expensive diamond rings. Winkle picker shoes — the latest fashion, but looking ancient. Nothing looked appealing or as though anybody would want it. The shop must have made money though, because when it was closed grilled shutters were down over the big plate glass windows. Andersons — J.G. Anderson, pawnbroker. Joseph Garibaldi. I only know this because several years later I knew his nephew. ('Uncle Joe — he's worth a bob or two. Joseph Garibaldi — don't laugh, that's nothing, they've all got those names. My Auntie Flo is Florence Nightingale Anderson and my Uncle Bill is William Gladstone Anderson.')

* * *

One Saturday evening I got back late and found Jean hanging out of my bedroom window at the front.

'There's a fight in the street,' she said, moving over to make room for me. Along both sides of the street many of the front doors were open, light flooding from them, people on their steps. A man and a woman were berating another woman in a threatening way, screaming at her and delivering the odd blow. It was horrible because she was alone and small and they were big and together. From what they said she had been babysitting for them. Suddenly I realised, 'Oh God — it's Dolly.' I ran down the two flights of stairs to ring the police. When I clambered back up the police car had arrived and Jean said 'They knocked her down and a youth came out of a house and said "Come on Mum," and helped her up and they went inside.' When the police car came, all the front doors shut. Dolly didn't come in the Bookshop for several weeks after this incident.

In the summer dark the sash window in my room was open wide to the night and the sounds of St Ann's. The football season had finished but the songs went on in the dark hot streets, gangs of youths went round late singing:

> Ay ay ay ay Grummit is better than Yashin
> Baker is better than Eusebio
> And Swindon/whoever are in for a thrashin'

echoing round on Friday and Saturday nights.

* * *

Jackie visited and she slept in my room and we chatted all night, periodically sitting up and eating snacks. 'You've both obviously been reared on school stories, where the girls have merry japes and midnight feasts in the dorm,' said Julian, his rest disturbed. He said when we were together we both started a third of our sentences with 'Nessie says...'

Jackie got on well with Pat, each time she visited her speech was decorated with his old slang from last time. 'Hello there, you crabs,' she would greet us heartily. 'Hey, mate-onovitch…'

There were film festivals at the Coop Film Theatre, from the New Wave, Godard and Robbe-Grillet and Bresson, and Italian and Spanish films.

* * *

We went to Sherwood Forest and Dick brought his fierce little six-year-old Sophia. 'Where's his hair?' she demanded, on seeing Pat.

* * *

John and Katherine came back from their honeymoon. John found a place on an old map called Lambley Dumble, it wasn't too far and we walked there with a picnic. It turned out to be just a field with blackberry bushes. We sunbathed and John and Chris planned a new board game, to be called *The Struggle*, based on *Snakes and Ladders*.

'You've taken my ham sandwich,' Bonnie complained to Julian. 'There was one each and you've had two.'

'Oh well,' he shrugged, at ease with the situation.

'No — that's my sandwich and I'll have the rest of it.' Bonnie was intransigent. He handed over the half-eaten sandwich and took a cheese one.

'You have just read the *Communist Manifesto*,' intoned Chris, ignoring the ill-will over the sandwich, 'and you now have your feet firmly on the road to Socialism. You can move up to the next area of struggle.'

'And what about, "You have failed to support your union's heroic industrial action — go right back to the beginning?"' offered John.

'And "Well done — you have written a leaflet explaining the dialectic so the working class can understand it, and it is proving very popular. Move up to square forty."'

'Just a minute — that sounds as though workers are thick or something — lots of people don't understand the dialectic,' objected Dave.

'Oh okay — "so everyone can understand it."'

Julian, with a meaningful look at Chris, said, 'Miss a turn because you have been temporarily led astray by the smart-arse elitist drivellings of a Cambridge don.'

The final one they decided must be, 'Well done! You have achieved the Dictatorship of the Proletariat. Welcome to the Workers Paradise.'

'No — the last one should be — "You will make your fortune marketing this board game, and will abandon fighting for the Revolution."'

'Oh no!' everybody cried out, and Martin rolled round laughing.

We sunbathed some more and then picked blackberries to take back to the Bookshop for a blackberry crumble, to put with apples and pears so it was big enough for everybody.

* * *

The Bay Horse on the corner of Alfred Street Central and Hutchinson Street was our pub for a long time. It was just across the road from the cobbled alley at the back of Dane Street. We sometimes went there very early. We tried to keep records with a fine political content on the jukebox — 'Blowin in the Wind' sung by Peter, Paul and Mary, 'If I Had a Hammer' by Trini Lopez, 'Midnight in Moscow' played by Kenny Ball and his Jazzmen — a jazzed up version of 'Under Moscow Skies'.

There were occasional meetings upstairs in the Bay Horse addressed by speakers from the Fourth International — Pierre Frank, Ernest Mandel, Eric Ernstzen. But things went sour eventually, Pat and Nancy the landlady had words over something or other. We were no longer welcome and had to wait ages to be served.

There was a wholesale decampment to the Princess Royal, which stood at the end of Northumberland Street — not conveniently near. It was a quiet pub and the landlady welcomed us with open arms. She made a big fuss of Jean whom she called 'Tiffany Jones' after a supposed likeness to a strip cartoon heroine in a daily paper. It's a mystery how she became a landlady, she was nervous of the area and said when she went to post a letter on Union Road in the afternoons she ran all the way back in her carpet slippers, not wanting to be in St Ann's streets late, and she wouldn't venture a foot out of doors after the local post left at 4.45. The Princess Royal was a large gloomy pub with few customers and no jukebox, and would have been suitably renamed the Mary Celeste. But the landlady was grateful for our custom.

At the weekends we often went to the Union Stewards Club on Gordon Road. It was absolutely packed out and there was live music.

The Bricklayers' Arms was in Lewis Street, the next street. A favourite of mine was the Freeman's Arms on the diagonal corner between Alfred Street Central and Great Freeman Street. There were two rooms downstairs and — a must in winter — a lovely fire. If it was perishing cold at home people went to the pub for warmth and company.

The Oliver Cromwell was a big pub on the corner of St Ann's Well Road and Alfred Street Central. We didn't go there, but we would have done had we known it was where the Nottingham branch of the First International had met, in the 1880s.

The Napoleon on St Ann's Well Road was old, dusty and silent. But deadly. It had a reputation — if you looked at another customer the wrong way you might get knifed. We only went in there once and we felt daring, but nothing happened. There was no jukebox and no conversation. Customers sat totally silent with their beers.

Round the corner on St Ann's Well Road at the back of a cobbled court was an enclave of Glaswegians presided over by Tricia. They lived in a big tumble-down flat, with curiously shaped rooms. Tiger, Patrick Mullaney and Vinnie were the ones I remember. They came down to Nottingham to get jobs. Pat maintained they had come to attempt to poach IG members. 'But they won't succeed,' he said definitely. They were all what was known as Selbyites — they took the political position of Harry Selby. Anyway, they crossed the road to drink in the Admiral Dundas. That was their pub. A rumour went round that it operated a colour bar, but they stoutly refuted it, and stuck up for the landlords with gusto. Dick and myself went there. It was absolutely jam-packed, people were stiff up to the bar like sardines. Other comrades were there too — George Powe and Jill and I think maybe Bob Gregory. We were served I think eventually — I'm not sure.

One pub that definitely had a colour bar was the Mechanics Arms on Alfred Street North. It was an ongoing issue for years. Alfonso and Steve made their way there on a summer evening, giving the Westminster pub a miss and going to Do Their Bit for the struggle. Pushing the door open, Alfonso knew he was straight into conflict, but it had to be done. The week before George Powe had tipped up someone's pint deliberately as a protest at not being served, and there was a steady succession of protests. When Jean and Dick weren't served, Jean and I went up in the middle of the night with a tin of red gloss paint and wrote RACIST PUB. By the next morning the pub's cream wall was completely clear, not a smear of red. They must have been alert there twenty-four hours a day. Across the road the youths in the Boys' Brigade all flooded to the dusty windows as two shrieking police cars arrived once more at the Mechanics Arms.

The Chase Tavern was further along St Ann's Well Road, across from Robin Hood Chase. We went in the small backroom, its jukebox with a big selection of Brenda Lee records. On the way home we went to the Italian chip shop next door, where the cooking oil was sweet and distinctive — maybe chestnut oil?

Another place to drink in was the Firemen's Club. They were on twenty-four hour call but most of the time were waiting, so they had their own social club, the bar was open long hours. We had cordial relations with the FBU and two of their firemen, Arthur Tideswell and Leo Keeley, took *The Bulletin* and then *The Week*. Leo was very agreeable and looked like an ageing matinée idol. Arthur was a smashing guy, he was close to us politically. I'm not sure he was in the Group, but he was definitely a sympathiser. Firemen had to be young and strong, so retirement came at forty-five, and Arthur was waiting to retire so he could go off to Fircroft College.

The main city Police Station and the Fire Station were in the same huge building near Milton Street, each having a corner, with an opening from which the fire engines left.

We went to their social club intermittently. When I first lived in Nottingham Dave Ablitt and I went. It was unusually quiet in there and I was moping over a man I was keen on in the IS and we were talking about him, and discussing the imminent bust-up on the *Young Guard* editorial board between us and the IS. Dave said I'd spent the entire evening crying into my beer and l always showed him up in pubs. One time I'd met him in a pub, eating an ice-cream and he went on and on about it. Obviously it was against a drinking man's etiquette to go in a pub eating ice-cream.

Anyway on this night l was drunk and we went to see Arthur in the control room which looked out from the corner across to Milton Street.

'Yes, these are all the controls here,' said Arthur, rather unwisely as it turned out. 'These switches fetch the engines out and these…' I surveyed the sloping board, much wider and not vertical like a switchboard, and listened closely to Arthur. All these switches, all this power in one place. I never truly felt before the giddiness of power and couldn't resist, was drunk anyway and began maniacally throwing and pulling all the switches I could reach. Alarm bells went off and then more bells. Arthur started laughing and Ieapt at my hands to stop them and sent someone downstairs to stop the fire engines leaving the station.

We strolled back to the Bookshop in the hot summer night, Dave complaining I'd showed him up again.

* * *

The last time I saw Nessie she rang me one Saturday out of the blue. We hadn't met for a while and the Youngs had had another baby, a little boy. She was visiting Nottingham with the Pendrys, they were taking her to the new Nottingham Playhouse as a treat, she'd been so unwell with the baby. Would I meet them in the Playhouse bar afterwards? Yes, of course I'd love to see her. She said I knew the Pendrys, they had lived in Derby at one time, he was now an MP. Tom Pendry hadn't been to the YS often, just looked in now and again as it were. He never voted on anything and seemed as though he was watching us cannily. He seemed a lot older. He sometimes brought Moira who worked for Derby Borough Council. They were engaged for about forty years, then they married and after about another forty years finally produced a weeny little baby. Well there was a big fuss christening the child, Elsie Tanner was the baby's godmother, wearing a big hat, and the photo was in all the papers.

When I met up with them Nessie looked the same. Moira hadn't changed either, although I didn't know her well. Anyway we exchanged gossip and Moira was complaining about Alan Mullarkey.

'An absolute fantasist, it's his poor wife I feel sorry for…' Alan had been good-looking and personable and was voted the first national chairman of the Young Socialists. He seemed destined for a career as an MP. But Tom, who said little and only came sometimes, had made it.

As the evening drew to a close I was in a quandary — should I ask them back to the Bookshop? Nessie was used to anything, but I wasn't sure how Pat would react to a right-wing MP.

'I'd like to ask you in but I'm not sure what's going on.'

'Don't worry Sylvia, it's all right,' said Nessie.

Just as well. When I opened the back door Pat ran downstairs and wouldn't let me go up, he said he'd given our beds to 'some comrades from an Arab tendency. We have some disagreements but are talking turkey with them in the kitchen.'

'Pat, you swine, is there an Arab in my bed now?'

'No.'

'Then why can't I come up and get something from my room?'

'You can't. These are very delicate negotiations. Go away.' He stood several steps up, completely blocking the stairs.

God knows what Jean did when she came back — she and Dick sometimes went to a shebeen on Saturday night anyway. Chris probably went to Tricia's round the corner. I telephoned John and Kathy to cadge a bed and with a sigh of resignation set off to walk all the way up Carlton Road about two in the morning. Thank goodness it was summer and a warm night.

When I arrived back the next day the Arabs had gone and I never saw them. My unknown guest had left my room tidy, tidier than I had left it.

About a year later we did have an Arab member in Nottingham IG — Mark — but he joined as a student, he wasn't one of those who came that night. He married one of our members, Lindsay, and they had a baby boy.

* * *

At the end of the summer like Despina, Chris, who had eaten of the Leavisite teacakes, had to return to Cambridge. Katherine had a letter from him:

> Dear Kathy,
> Please collect my jacket from the cleaners and send it to me. A postal order for 8/- is enclosed.
> Many thanks, Yours, Chris

'Typical,' said Pat. Kathy fortunately thought it was funny and didn't mind a bit.

Jean brought back mugs from her holiday for us — black, brown and cream stripes, one each for Pat, herself and me.

By the end of the school holidays anybody dialling 999 Fire Brigade about a kitten in a tree received the testy response, 'Then you'll have to get it yourself, we're not coming out again.' The picnics ended, the students came back, the Labour Party conference loomed.

1968

We were all thrilled to bits about the events in Paris in May 1968 when it exploded with demos and sit-ins and strikes and non-stop meetings.

At the time I was at a Rehabilitation Centre in Long Eaton on a month-long course, sent by my psychiatrist and suggested to me by Mrs Tate. We were split into groups of about six. In our group there were four ex-miners who had been made redundant due to ill-health, a girl called Angela Guy and myself. Angela had been in the Civil Service and was off sick because she had begun seeing things that weren't there. This was labelled 'confusion'. She was twenty-seven and lived with her parents in the suburbs.

We had simple lessons — basic Maths and English, some sort of physical work with our hands, metalwork perhaps — in the mornings with a man who was our instructor, or group leader. Other groups were in different sheds with their own instructors. In the mornings too we had coffee together as a group. The miners were mostly in their fifties and surprisingly placid, quite unlike the popular idea of stroppy miners. 'He didn't mean any harm,' or, 'He means well,' they would say and they would look reproachful at any criticism of the staff. The exception was the youngest ex-miner, who was about forty and more abrasive. 'Well, she's a waste of space,' he said of the psychologist, whom we all saw individually twice a week. The other miners looked sad at this and shook their heads — 'She's doing her best.'

At lunchtime everybody went to the main building to eat. In the afternoons we worked in the gardens with everyone else who was there, hoeing between potatoes and carrots in rectangles of ground. Angela and I became friendly with John. He was a young married man, tall and beautiful, with dark eyes and golden-brown curly hair, wearing a purple shirt open nearly to the waist and showing a gold tan. We were all tanned that May, it was boiling hot and we were out under the sun every afternoon.

Normally good looks don't do much for me, I seek more than that in a man, but John was so kind to a little girl in his group. She was small with a bent back, and he teased her and spoke gently to her. 'Oh, Glenda's really come out of her shell with John,' said a lady classmate.

Glenda looked expectantly for him and he never let her down or was abrupt. 'Hello — come on, get hoeing and if you make it up to there I'll finish the row.' She sparkled with delight when he teased her, and he fetched her a drink in the afternoon break.

'There you are, that'll keep you going, all that talking you've been doing,' he said, handing her a mug. 'She hardly spoke at all before John bothered with her,' observed the middle-aged lady. She didn't actually say a lot.

I liked John very much and lots of people did. We didn't get paid for hoeing rows, but you felt obliged to do a respectable amount.

Every morning a coach picked everybody up in the Market Square and took us to the Long Eaton centre. It took us back to the Square about four o'clock. On Fridays we had to hand in an essay on a subject given to us. In the third week the subject was 'Where I would most like to be'. Well of course that May 1968 my essay went something like, 'Right now I would most like to be in Paris, where the working class is on the move, together with students they are trying to make a whole new society where humanity matters. They are demonstrating and making intelligent demands of their government…' After marking, our instructor handed them back. He said drily to me and without much enthusiasm, 'I can't find any mistakes so it's ten out of ten.'

On Friday afternoons we finished early, and after the coach had dropped everybody back in the Square, Angela, John and myself went for a drink and a chat in Lyons Café. Angela was planning a seaside holiday before she looked for another job. 'I don't want the civil service again. Anything in an office, or even something completely different if it crops up.'

John agreed, 'Yes, I don't mind what I do, I'll do anything.' He shrugged his shoulders good-naturedly. 'My uncle says he might have some work for me,' he finished vaguely.

One Friday three young men came in as we were mulling over the day, and they hailed John. They came to sit with us and as they were talking one of them said keenly 'Hey, last Saturday night we chased a bunch of Africans through town and all the way up Hockley and we managed to cut some of them.' It was a strange expression, but that's what he said.

Angela and I looked horrified; John was embarrassed and started talking about something else.

'Well then, you should be thoroughly ashamed of yourself,' I piped up.

The young man looked straight back at me in a hostile manner and demanded belligerently of John, 'Where did you meet her — Sunday school?'

Both he and I turned to John for an explanation of the other, but he was looking at the ceiling. They pushed off and we saw Angela onto her bus and then started the trek towards St Ann's.

'How do you know him?' I demanded, as we walked along Parliament Street and through Victoria black tunnel, and down Union Road.

'I don't know him, he's just… around.' He shrugged and lifted his arms in a disclaimer of responsibility.

'Well he's appalling. I hope you don't listen.'

'Well but you've got some funny ideas. I mean, I come from business people, and they don't think like you.'

'Hello John. How's Marlene?' asked a passing girl, casting a sharp eye over me.

'She's okay, go round and see her, she'll like to see you,' he replied, pleasantly enough, but not looking at her and not stopping his heavy measured tread, his canvas bag across his shoulder.

'That Bookshop — they've got funny ideas there.'

'I've never seen you in the Bookshop.'

'I don't have much call for books, don't read, don't have time.'

'But there are comics as well.'

'Well I count that as reading, don't have time for them either.'

Although he lived round the corner from the top of Dane Street I'd never seen John before; he must have gone to different pubs. After the course finished I only saw him again once. It was December of the same year, early evening, the dark lively with bustle on Alfred Street Central. John was staring intently into a second-hand furniture shop, a longing in his dark eyes that suggested more than tables and chairs. Was he seeing his home at Christmas with his small children? How was little Glenda now? — she wouldn't be seeing him. Somehow heartbreak was bound into him. The weak light from the shop bulb showed the furniture and his beautiful face and the longing in his dark eyes.

* * *

In the wake of the events in Paris that summer we had quite a few student visitors to Nottingham from the JCR (*Jeunesse Communiste Révolutionaire*), the youth section of the Fourth International. The ones I remember most were Marie-Hélène, from the south, and Marina. Marie-Hélène's parents were both head teachers and she had been at the Sorbonne when it erupted, as had Marina. She came from Normandy and her parents had a dog called a griffon. Marina's real name was Anneke Huguet, but she adored everything Russian and had chosen to be called a Russian name. She had put in to spend her year away from the Sorbonne in Leningrad, but there was an administrative mix up and the poor thing was sent to Leek, northern Staffordshire. We all thought this was funny and sang:

Oh Mr Porter
It really is a cheek
She wanted to go to Leningrad
But they sent her off to Leek.

Most weekends she came to Nottingham and stayed over at Julian's.

We had intense discussions on how society should be organised, asked how the countries we lived in — ostensibly free — could be truly free when they oppressed other countries. At weekends Julian sat translating the latest from French — Althusser and Derrida. I found them difficult to understand even in English. Derrida said we must imagine another world and it would become possible. This idea was everywhere then, and when John Lennon's 'Imagine' was released we understood.

One night of that summer stands out in my mind. Marie-Hélène and I had been at the Gortons babysitting their little girl Megan. The Gortons were Toni and Frank, they had come to Nottingham from Toronto, and were both in the Fourth International and the IG in Nottingham, active in their unions, and Toni was prominent in the local women's movement.

Marie-Hélène and I were walking back to town from their home in West Bridgford. The buses had all finished and we went over Trent Bridge and along Arkwright Street, deserted and silent. She was talking about her course and enthusing over D.H. Lawrence, her delight unbounded. She said how passionately she loved his work, how liberating it was for her and how there was no-one in French literature like him. We agreed that at his best Lawrence was the peak, and both of us kept re-lighting the other's enthusiasm. 'I can't believe I'm here where he lived,' she said passionately.

'I love to go to the library. It's a Victorian building. Lawrence attended it, it was part of the university then.'

'Oh you'll have to show me,' she cried.

There were few passers-by in the summer night, all the road and the night belonged to us and our enthusiasm swooped into pinnacles and throbbed with possibilities.

When I mentioned Lawrence to Marina it produced a vastly different response. 'Oh him. He goes on and on, what a windbag.' I found myself partially agreeing with her — well it's true, he does go on and on.

‘But at his very best don’t you think he’s wonderful?’ Because that’s true too.

Marina uttered a pouf of dismissal.

* * *

In 1968 *If...* was shown at the Savoy Cinema in Lenton. I was bowled over. Julian liked it but thought it was probably escapism.

‘Was it like your public school?’

‘Er, not quite. We didn’t take to the roof with guns. But it was very militarised. It was founded by a fighting bishop — Odo, William the Conqueror’s Archbishop of Canterbury. He wasn’t allowed to shed blood so he blipped people with a great club, not a sword.’

Then there was an Italian film festival at the Coop Film Theatre. When we went to see *Theorem* Martin Turner was there brimming over with his usual enthusiasm. The lights went out and we watched as a beautiful stranger seduced all the members of a family — father, mother, son, daughter, maid. Afterwards everybody clamoured to state their views. The consensus was it showed the disintegration of the bourgeois family.

‘Only the maid can survive, because the proletariat has vitality and faith,’ a youth pointed out.

‘But the maid is peasant, not proletarian.’

There had been boos from the audience when the maid levitated.

‘What do you think?’ asked Martin.

‘The father would survive too — he tore all his clothes off on the railway station, unpeeling the layers of bourgeois deceit and giving up everything,’ I said.

‘There are some Italian students now in the Labour club at Oxford, I’ll ask them what they think.’ Martin promised.

* * *

In 1968 we had an irrepressible hope in the future and turned towards the rest of the world with enthusiasm, not fear. I don’t think we were happy — young people usually aren’t. We took the terrible events in Vietnam greatly to heart. Yet an infectious spirit of gaiety was everywhere. The Beatles’ song ‘All you need is Love’ permeated the 1960s and we believed it. Some of us still do.

Enoch Powell was mouthing off from the mid 1960s, giving his ‘Rivers of Blood’ speech in 1968.

‘Oh God,’ said Dick glumly. ‘Listen to him. What am I going to tell my little black children?’

That summer Powell was invited to a public meeting at a school in Nottinghamshire in the evening, which was hard to get to. They probably didn’t want to risk a meeting in the city. Cars and vans full of people went to protest and shriek ‘Sieg Heil’ and smack his car as it drove to the school entrance up a leafy lane. About five of us — I didn’t know the others — hurried round the building, thinking he’d leave by the back after the meeting. This is what happened. He was bundled into a car at the back of the school, ashen-faced and not looking at anybody. None of us shouted anything but we stood with placards ‘One race — the human race.’

The nervousness of that time isn’t always remembered now. After Julian moved back to Nottingham I went round there and watched TV sometimes, including the tennis that summer. There was an American tennis player then called Peaches Bartkowicz who was quite successful. Lovely Dan Maskell and Jack Kramer were the commentators and there was a feel of gentle sportsmanship in the grass. One time after tennis the news came on, with a horrible photo of ranting Enoch Powell, mouth snarling and eyes rolling. ‘Oh look,’ said Julian, ‘it’s Peaches Powell.’ This mildly amusing remark occasioned paroxysms of laughter in me, the most I ever remember. I clutched my stomach and dropped tears, which I can only attribute to a big dose of nerves. Powell was extremely threatening, he promised a bloodbath and our society in ruins.

That year the Queen’s Christmas talk was about the Commonwealth and all the different and worthwhile people she had met from various backgrounds, and their contribution to the general good. It was a salve on the festering sore of racism and helped calm things down in society.

* * *

As winter set in Marina dressed in long-johns and flannel underwear her mother gave her for Christmas. ‘Oh zis country, so cold, so wet, oh my God I freeze.’ When she slept on the sofa she pulled it right next to the gas fire which was full on.

By the late 1960s the character of demos seemed to have changed. They were bigger, dense with noise, demonstrators packed closer together, pacifist contingents absent. There were usually groups from the continent. ‘We are all/Foreign scum,’ we chanted after newspapers had complained ‘foreign scum’ would be present.

We shall fight
We will win
Paris London Rome Berlin.

Because the demos were more organised than in the early days we went in hired coaches and didn't have to leave early. So they were longer, larger, darker. Bertrand Russell sent messages of support read out over a microphone, his physical presence no longer there. Demonstrations became generally more aggressive. We linked arms to break police lines. With the arms lifted up your body was more exposed and afterwards you felt as though you had been thrashed, necessitating hot baths for about a week.

'Meet the Vietnamese in London', said the sticker for the March 1968 demo. Female representatives from the NLF spoke over the microphone, as did Tariq and Vanessa Redgrave, who gave out white crepe headbands for demonstrators to wear, a symbol of mourning in Vietnam. As more and more people streamed into Trafalgar Square, thousands and thousands, Pat cackled with laughter 'Look — it's like the Sorcerer's Apprentice.'

The day was long, and booths and vans were selling drinks, snacks and ice-cream at wildly inflated prices. We marched to the US embassy and were still there as it grew dark. The massive embassy with its eagle reared up, bare flat lawn in front and hundreds of police. I became separated from the Nottingham contingent and bumped into Jackie, and when police on horseback started charging the crowds in the dark there was nowhere to go, there were so many people you could barely move.

We held hands in the surge and made in the direction of the trees, holding round a trunk, presuming the mounted police wouldn't charge it. Wearing slip-on shoes was insane, you could hear girls shrieking their shoes were lost; police helmets flew up into the air; a guy was poking the white flank of a horse with a pole and we started shouting at him and another girl joined in. He was carried away in the crowds with his pole… Rumours abounded, passed about like wildfire in the pitch dark.

'There's a gun in the embassy trained on the entrance, they'll shoot if anybody breaks through…'

'Sean Kelly's stomach has been stamped on by a police horse…'

'Sean Kelly's stomach…'

'Sean Kelly's stomach…'

Who was Sean Kelly? The embassy lights glittered through the trees and the darkness.

There were many injuries and mass arrests. Afterwards it was known as the Battle of Grosvenor Square.

In the spring the Tet offensive showed it was unlikely the US could win the war, yet the bombing continued, with thousands more Vietnamese civilians slaughtered. Another demo was planned for October. Pat and the organisers were determined it shouldn't be hijacked by violent protesters and argued against it going to the American embassy.

The authorities were deeply alarmed by the impending October demo, both because of the violence in March at Grosvenor Square, and because in May in Paris that year demonstrators had taken over the streets for weeks and were supported by the trade unions. The newspapers and the television were warning and apocalyptic. In an increasingly alarmist media Ralph Miliband, a sponsor of *The Week*, spoke up in favour of protests in a free society, and suggested there be no police on the streets, as this had led to the March violence. This was backed up by Tariq, who spoke at length in the media on it. Amazingly this was taken on board, and the police presence was cut right down.

The demo was to assemble on the Embankment, take a letter to Harold Wilson at Downing Street, and then move on to Hyde Park for the speeches. At 2pm there were thousands and thousands, and thousands still coming. Pat and the other organisers suspected anarchists and Maoists would probably try to divert the demonstrators to the US embassy, and provoke violence. On the day Tariq and others were ready with microphones, encouraging people to carry on up to Downing Street. Some people still went along a side street to the US embassy but few followed them, and it must have fizzled out. After the letter was handed in the march made its way to Hyde Park. Hours and hours later demonstrators were still flooding in to the park…

It was the biggest demonstration ever, and it was peaceful. The numbers involved must have influenced Harold Wilson to refuse to send British troops to Vietnam. The protesters were right and Wilson was right to listen to them. Had the US administration taken on board this lesson it would have been well. It was an object lesson in practical politics, and how the people should be listened to and not intimidated.

* * *

That year the South African ambassador was unwise enough to visit Nottingham, I think at the invitation of the university Monday Club — and received a tumultuous reception. Mayhem reigned in town at the meeting, the police were everywhere and there were arrests. Eventually three people were charged with affray and had to appear in the magistrates' court the following January. The court was full of various people of the left, as well as from university and the press. Most IG members were at work (which contradicts the idea we only had students) but one of our members, Brian Davey was charged, so Marina and I went.

The first defendant was Chris something, I've forgotten his surname, he was a young Maoist with a girlfriend called Shahida and they often turned up to public meetings and protests. I don't remember the Maoists as much of a force in Nottingham then. Chris gave his testimony clearly and without comment or attitude, and after he had testified he joined the observers in the court, sitting on the front row. He then ostentatiously opened the *Little Red Book* and sat reading from it, ignoring the proceedings in court. What wonderful concentration! There wasn't much evidence against him, as I recall. It went over into the second day, and Brian was the first in court. I was mad at Marina because she was ages in the bathroom putting blushes on her cheeks and I thought we'd miss it. 'Marina — come *on,*' — I banged on the bathroom door.

We'd only missed a little bit. With his high cheekbones and scornful manner Brian looked the very picture of student arrogance, and I worried this would affect the magistrates adversely. The prosecuting counsel was very hostile and said briskly, 'You've heard the testimony of Mr Piers Something, who said you ran down the corridor screaming and causing trouble, and you hit a policeman.'

Brian looked haughty and replied 'He's a liar.'

There was a frisson of alarm in the court at the intransigence. The cheekbones got higher and obviously no emollience was to be expected. He gave the impression he wasn't going to lower himself by going into details about events. The counsel got more annoyed.

'I don't think so, Mr Piers Something is a well-respected student and I suggest it's you who are the liar.'

'That would be completely untrue.'

Professor Sheila Something was called for the defence, Brian's tutor. She found it hard to believe he would act in that way, she said, he had a greatly developed moral sense and was a brilliant student. Personally I couldn't see this doing him much good with magistrates.

The third defendant was Steve Sparatsu. The court relaxed, he was well-known on the left if only by reputation — as a Jamaican wild man who broke places up.

Dick would pull his head into his shoulders like a tortoise at the mention of his name, and Pat would instruct before leaving, 'Well I'm off. The duplicator isn't mine if the bailiffs come, and if Steve Sparatsu knocks in the middle of the night for fuck's sake don't open the door.' ('Pat isn't here,' I'd shouted down into the darkness when Steve Sparatsu crashed on the door, 'and I can't open the door, it's jammed.')

He looked fairly ordinary in the daylight. Before being cross-questioned he held up a stern finger at the court. 'I'd like to say one thing. I'm absolutely against violence.'

Smirks abounded at this statement. His name was spelled Soparatsua which caused no end of problems for the counsels and mostly they just gave up on it mid-sentence. 'Mr Sopa… Sop… Sop… the defendant.'

During the adjournment we wandered into the court entrance and studied the list of offences to be tried. Most of them were for petty theft or for 'being a common prostitute'. Was this a crime?

'It shouldn't be,' weighed in a man with a beard, who held forth on the state's hypocrisy. What was the difference between a common and an uncommon prostitute? Calling the girls this was like adding insult to injury.

Back in the court we waited for the verdict. I thought they would all be found guilty. Marina shook her head, unable to pronounce on proceedings in an English court. A boy in the next row explained carefully, 'Either that or they'll all be let off. They can't find the English ones not guilty and the Jamaican guilty. It will look like racism.' But that's what they did.

* * *

In 1968 too there was a big civil rights march in Derry, Northern Ireland. Catholics there were discriminated against in housing and jobs. After partition from Catholic Éire (1921), Northern Ireland was created to ensure a permanent Protestant Unionist majority. They won every election and in order to sustain this majority gerrymandering took place in council elections, housing was allocated to Protestants but not Catholics, even where in some towns they were a majority.

In 1968 all over the world the young were protesting, the light of freedom in their eyes, and the countries' power structures were big and unwillingly generous enough to absorb the protests. The exception was Northern Ireland, which slammed down brutally on its young people's hopes, with disastrous and tragic consequences.

Derry Housing Association joined with the local Labour Party and organised rent strikes and protests. After May 1968, inspired by the Paris students, People's Democracy was formed. They organised a march in late 1968 when a few hundred marchers went into the Protestant area of Derry and were met with great violence by the police (the RUC — Royal Ulster Constabulary) who beat them with truncheons and drove them back into the Catholic ghetto. Early in 1969 a Belfast to Dublin Civil Rights March was attacked by paramilitary police. Inside Derry barricades went up in the Bogside and the police were unable to get in for several days.

Nottingham IMG decided to hold a public meeting on the Irish Civil Rights struggle. Posters went up and Irish pubs like the Hand in Heart in town were leafleted. It was to be held in the Great Lecture Hall at the university. Speakers came from People's Democracy — Eamonn McCann, Bernadette Devlin and Bowes Egan, a young Protestant lawyer. In the early days it was the policy of People's Democracy to always have a speaker on the platform who was Protestant and sympathetic to civil rights. (Later when things hardened that became impossible.)

The lecture hall was bursting and there were masses outside who couldn't get in. Many had come to hear Bernadette, she was in the news a lot then and was fantastically popular, she was MP for Mid Ulster.

It turned out to be the biggest public meeting in Nottingham for a very long time. The speakers described what had happened on the peaceful demos, of the RUC brutality and the history since 1921. They were socialist and campaigned for better housing for all workers, Catholic and Protestant. Their grievances were absolutely legitimate and they had a vision of how things might be otherwise for everybody.

After the meeting we all went back to Julian's — the speakers and Brian, Marina and two teenage girls (Moira and Roisin) from the Catholic Teacher Training College in Nottinghamshire. Bernadette was fine, she fell in with arrangements ('I thought I might have a prima donna on my hands, but not at all,' said Julian, who had organised it). Later Marina told them about when the Sorbonne erupted.

Afterwards the IMG had acquired some more sympathisers. I sent a note to Moira and Roisin asking them to tea with cream cakes one Friday evening. They sent a polite note back, saying they couldn't come.

Julian barked out laughter — 'The nuns won't let them out.'

The Split

Each week Pat came from London brimming with enthusiasm for all the new people he had met, especially Tariq Ali — 'Oh he's a great guy,' Ernie and Jess. Jerry Lawless. 'What a fantastic name.' 'Yes and he's a fantastic guy.' Ray Sparrow. Bob Purdie. We didn't see any of them, except Tariq eventually, and Ernie.

'Vanessa and Corin Redgrave will be there,' Pat announced about a forthcoming London anti-war event, 'so I expect we'll get those little cucumber sandwiches with the crusts cut off.' He was disappointed when they joined the SLL.

* * *

Ken rang. 'We're coming round now to take the ISJs (*International Socialist Journal*).'

'What, all of them?' I said.

'Yes, all of them. They're not yours,' Ken said sharply.

'Ken, you're living in fantasy land if you think I covet these ISJs. They're the most boring thing I ever read.'

'They're not boring,' he replied indignantly.

'Well if you're going to take all of them you'll need a car, they're heavy and there's lots of them.'

Ken came round with somebody in a car and they piled the ISJs in and off they went. I didn't think anything of it. It didn't cross my mind it was the opening move at the start of a big split. When Pat came from London he was nonplussed and mildly annoyed and said, 'I don't think they belong to Ken either.'

I had many diverse and enchanting conversations with Ken, who could be wonderful company. But he could also be disposed to ticking people off. Pat remonstrated with him several times, saying he couldn't speak to voluntary workers as though they are employees. 'Most of them have done a day's work before coming here.'

Compared to other groups the IG/IMG didn't have many faction fights, but the monster one in the offing left devastation.

* * *

The Bertrand Russell Peace Foundation was run by Russell's secretary, the dynamic American Ralph Schoenman, and by Ken Coates and Chris Farley. There was some trouble in the Foundation but we only heard rumblings. ('It's like musical chairs round the money,' someone said.) Neither Pat nor Ken were interested in money for its own sake.

But then there was a monetary crisis in the Foundation which was generously funding several projects, including the VSC headquarters in London and twelve staff. In early 1968 the BRPF pulled the plug on the money and the offices from which a demo was being organised. There wasn't enough money in the bank; given how much money the BRPF was losing this was fair enough and inevitable but it caused trouble. We heard the staff were immediately locked out without notice. However, closure had apparently been in the pipeline since October 1967, according to a memo from Chris Farley, who said the staff must be given fourteen or twenty-eight days notice.

Ralph Schoenman wrote to Ernest Mandel on 12 April 1968: 'Pat and Geoff reacted to the request to economise by launching a campaign against Ken suggesting that because he had ambitions with bureaucrats in the trade union movement he feared militance of the VSC and wanted to kill it. This infantile slander is doubly ironic because Ken thought up the VSC.'

Ralph Schoenman was out of the country when it all blew up, and the authorities refused him entry back in on the grounds he constituted a risk to the state. This was at a time when Vietnam was being relentlessly bombed.

Ken had written to Pat on 14 October 1967: 'How can you possibly say that I "dislike taking a principled position on the Vietnam (war)?" Have you forgotten everything, how it was my initiative which got you appointed to the Foundation to launch the VSC? How it was my idea, and mine alone, to begin such a movement in Britain and how I persuaded Ralph to allow us to take on such a project alongside the Tribunal, and how that was how you came to work for the Foundation?'

Nottingham in those days was known on the left as Trottingham because of the density of Trotskyists on the ground, so lots of people were dragged into the faction fight. Documents and letters were flying back and forth, angry, worried, abusive, urgent… No-one was left untouched. It was ongoing and bitter. Comrades who supported Ken stopped coming round to the Bookshop. Ken was spoken of in certain circles as 'the renegade Coateski' echoing some long gone Soviet factional struggle.

Peter Price was terribly upset about the row. 'We can't let this happen. We must bring them together.' He went round visiting members individually, urging them to intervene on the side of harmony, and he arranged a meeting between Pat and Ken at Park Road.

Peter was one of the older triumvirate who, with Pat and Ken, had left the Communist Party in 1956 and joined the Labour Party, and then founded the International Group in 1962. Peter was pivotal to the Group's work in Nottingham, yet now he seems to have been forgotten. With his booming actor's voice and swinging duffel coat he was central to many struggles. The children's playground across Alfred Street was Peter's doing. 'There's nothing for the children round here. They must have a playground,' — he had got together with our councillor Jimmy Green and they pushed it through the Council. While Ken was writing a book on St Ann's poverty and Pat was running the Bookshop, Peter sorted the playground out, and supported a rather secretive actors' club a couple of streets away.

The meeting at Peter's wasn't a success. Perhaps too many spiteful letters had been exchanged by then. Both sides made statements. Pat said he and Geoff had arrived for work and found they were locked out, when a demonstration against an imperialist war was being organised that promised to be the biggest ever.

Ken said Pat and Geoff had ended up a long way from their Midlands roots. Finally and crucially he said there was a financial crisis in the BRPF which necessitated redundancies, there was no alternative to sacking. He spoke on condition there would be no questions, which infuriated some people.

I wasn't present at the meeting, Julian went and came back, 'These are the politics of the boardroom,' he tapped out on the typewriter in a document backing Pat.

I can't remember the letters that were exchanged and probably didn't see all of them. Pat's contributions would have been just as nasty as Ken's. The only letter I remember, and it caused great offence, was one from Ken with instructions to the people in London after the VSC offices were locked. 'These people are thieves and mustn't be let into the building on any pretext whatsoever.' The people he was speaking of were the comrades he had worked closely with for several years, and who had loyally defended him when he was being thrown out of the Labour Party in 1965.

We didn't see it but an item in the nebulously titled Scottish Report 27 October 1967 said: 'We should appropriate any piece of physical equipment, stationery, etc from the remains of this venture, extract the appropriate redundancy payments etc in the most unscrupulous fashion if necessary…' perhaps this was written by Pat and Geoff? If so, it contradicts the idea they didn't know about the impending redundancies, and perhaps explains Ken's attitude.

In the holidays Martin Turner came back from Oxford and he was here, there and everywhere, exploring. He supported Pat with considerable gusto. 'It's insane isn't it, how can he justify pulling the plug on the VSC when American imperialism is destroying a small country and there are thousands of people who want to register their protest?'

But then he'd go round and have a chat with Ken and come back. 'Well I can see Ken's point. He wants to build something permanent, not just a flash in the pan.'

'By a flash in the pan I take it you mean the Vietnam War?' Julian replied coolly.

Martin fussed about so much back and forth — perhaps he was trying to implement Peter's plea for harmony. But he earned the nickname 'Martin the Turn', said with guffaws of rude laughter. Such was Martin's good nature he took it cheerfully and nobody fell out with him. He went back to Oxford and we never saw him again. After receiving his degree he married an Italian student and went to live in Italy. The next we heard he had been sentenced to eight years in prison for robbing banks. He was, I believe, the only IMG member to take this path, although Alistair Darling became Chancellor of the Exchequer, so also handled large sums of money, but it wasn't quite the same as bank robbery.

* * *

Pat brought me a cup of tea in bed — the first time he'd been there for a week — and announced 'Bonnie's cleaning the kitchen.' Of course she is!

'Okay.'

Obviously I wasn't concerned enough, for he then said plaintively 'She's changing everything.'

'Well you're a Marxist, you can cope with that.'

Bonnie was Bonnie Oberman, her family lived round the corner from Jackie in Broadstairs. She'd left both the Rose Bruford School of Drama and then teacher training college, and wasn't sure yet what she wanted to do. Last heard of she was at LAMDA, but that was afterwards.

Pat came back later with another cup of tea. 'Now she's moved all the reference books and,' with a cunning expression, 'she's taken down the picture of Hugo Blanco.'

I got up and went downstairs. 'Now then, Bonnie, what's going on?'

'I'm just making a few… changes…' her voice faded.

'That's fine, you can put up anything you like but you can't take stuff down. Where is the picture of Hugo Blanco, the Peruvian peasant leader?'

We scrabbled about in the bin and I pulled it out. The chocolate spread was there too. 'That's Jean's. Property is theft, of course, but nobody else wants it anyway, and she'll look for it when she comes.'

Jean had put on a gown and mortar and gone off to eat strawberries and collect her degree. After that she obtained a teaching job in Leicester. She still kept her room at the Bookshop and at weekends she came back, and so did Dick, who drove over from Birmingham, where he was then at Fircroft College. Julian had moved back to Nottingham and he and Brian were teaching at People's College. Jean started a Women's Lib group in Leicester and I went one time. There were eight members and they were active and vocal, and personally supportive of one another in a way that IMG members were not. Two were single mothers and one was about to be. I was thrilled to be there, and about Women's Lib generally.

* * *

Trotsky is the very face of revolutionary ardour, yet I felt rather guilty for not liking him more.

'Trotsky was wonderful of course, where would the Revolution have been without him? But sometimes I don't like him very much,' I confessed to Julian, who let out a bark of laughter.

'It doesn't matter, we're not in a fan club.'

It was the Kronstadt sailors. The Russian navy was right behind the Revolution. How could he have had them shot? What a terrible precedent. He apologised afterwards — rather too late.

Nevertheless I still think Trotsky was right about the Permanent Revolution, that it has to be constantly fought. Is this so very different from Thomas Jefferson's 'The price of Liberty is eternal vigilance'?

Marx considered a peaceful revolution unlikely because the ruling class wouldn't allow it. But twenty-four years after the publication of the *Communist Manifesto* both Marx and Engels thought a revolution without bloodshed possible in Britain, that in developed countries labour may attain its goal by peaceful means. It might be so. And after all the Windsors aren't the Romanovs. The coronation postage stamp (with the nimbus of flowers round the Queen's head) was designed by

Marx's niece Enid Marx. That shows lack of prejudice on both sides. As William Morris said 'It isn't revenge we want for the workers, but happiness.'

Yet perhaps Marx would no longer believe that labour could triumph, since the trades unions were so depleted of power here in the 1980s. We need to begin to make workers' rights real again, for it was after the trades unions were weakened that the assault on the population intensified and our society became more fractured and unfair. People are encouraged to be scared of trade union power and that is wrong. There is ongoing militarism, poverty and homelessness, climate disruption and the rise of the vicious right, plus a huge gap between words and reality. If we want to rescue our society (and the planet) we must extend the network of democracy.

* * *

Pat shuffled through the post and handed me a letter.

'It's from Jackie. She's standing for Parliament,' I said.

'What!'

'In Thanet.'

'Good God, they must be absolutely desperate down there,' Pat said rudely, but he was really quite pleased about it.

'She writes, "My mother is going to make all my outfits with matching hats. We won't win the seat, but I'm going to put up a jolly good fight with a proper socialist programme."'

Pat made toast and Bonnie said, 'I don't think it's fair, Jackie can be Jewish but I can't.'

'Can't you convert?'

'No! I shouldn't have to. I'm an atheist anyway, so why would I convert?'

'Well I suppose I know what you mean. I'm C of E but I haven't done anything to be that, it wouldn't be the same.'

'It's passed through the mother and it's Jackie's mother who's Jewish and it's my father.'

'Well, you have a Jewish name and she doesn't.'

'There is that, I suppose,' replied Bonnie, reluctantly looking on the bright side.

* * *

Later in the week a big envelope came in the post for Bonnie. A cry came from her as she opened it. 'My mummy's sent some flowers from our garden.' She dropped a tear as she pulled out layers of damp newspaper and frail little stems — buttercups, Canterbury bells, pink flowers — maybe wild geranium — and an assortment of different daisies. She lifted the limp little bodies from the newspaper, weak from their precarious journey through the post. When put in a tumbler of water they revived wonderfully. 'Look what Bonnie's mummy's sent her.' Pat smiled approvingly at the flowers on the kitchen mantelpiece, under pictures of a panda and Hugo Blanco, and Theo Melville's batty letter accusing us all of political buffoonery.

Also enclosed in the envelope was a cutting from the front page of the Thanet paper — a photo of Jackie. 'Your Labour candidate Miss Jackie ('don't call me Jacqueline') Taylor.'

'God, how awful,' said Bonnie.

* * *

St Ann's stood waiting to be pulled down.

Of the customers, Bridget had grown older but not much bigger in size. She never came into the Bookshop again after the death of her brother. Dolly married one of the cheeky-daft Italians. The Misses Best were moved out to a council flat — a traumatic event for them, they had lived in that house as little girls. Goodness knows what happened to the Walkers. But one day I was on Castle Boulevard outside Julian's flat, and who should cycle by, presumably on his way to work, but Mr Walker. We both smiled and waved like mad — he nearly fell off his bike waving. St Ann's was down, that time was over, but we were both survivors and had known its rare quality.

* * *

Peter was right. The split was disastrous. It was a long time coming but it was devastating. The factionalism that characterised left splinter groups, and had been generally absent in the IG/IMG for several years, burst forth unchecked. Pat and Ken worked in different areas, they were complementary, so there needn't have been conflict. It's easy to say that now, but once it starts it's hard to stop.

In the weeks preceding the October 1968 demonstration the *Daily Mail* called Pat 'the most dangerous man in Britain', and the *Daily Express*, 14 October, wrote he was 'Founder of the VSC... an imaginative agitator with twenty years' political experience... a dedicated back-room plotter... never far from Tariq Ali's side at big marches...'

Pat was a seasoned faction fighter and the wonder is not that the split happened but that it didn't happen before. There was a long honeymoon, when the three of them — Pat, Ken and Peter — built the IG/IMG. Since leaving the Communist Party in 1956 they had worked solidly and loyally together.

Yet although the split was felt to be devastating, perhaps it should be seen as part of the natural world, for a seed splits as it has to in irder to disperse.

Afterwards both Pat and Ken pursued their own work. Pat stayed in London and took part in local Labour Party politics and worked for the Fourth International — he was part of their Africa Commission — until his spectacular fall from grace.

Ken did so many things it's hard to record them briefly — founded the Russell Press, which continued until 2018, became a Labour MEP, continued to arrange Workers' Control conferences.

* * *

One Saturday in 1966 Ken, Peter, Bob and Brian banged at the Bookshop door. Julian went down to answer it and came back saying they had come to take the duplicator to the new office, on Mansfield Road. I knew nothing about it and Pat wasn't there, which he usually was on a Saturday. He was still paying for it, I think, and didn't know about its removal until afterwards. *The Week* would continue to be collated and sent out on Wednesdays but from the new office. Goodness knows who was paying the rent for it, possibly the Peace Foundation or maybe Peter, who sometimes, l believe, dug deep into his pockets. *The Bulletin* and then *The Week* had been put together, duplicated, collated and sent out for four years from Dane Street, and the Bookshop was never quite the same without the duplicator, although the typing and editing still went on there. About six months later the whole enterprise moved to London.

So let's leave the Bookshop at New Year, 1966. Refusing to acknowledge Christmas, Pat ran round in the January sales snatching presents quickly for his parents, a novel by Mrs Gaskell for Jean, a scarf for Julian, a 1966 page-a-day diary for me (it records that Pat and Tony Southall came round on the evening of the 1st January). Festivity in St Ann's wasn't quite over, for across the night rooftops on her broomstick flies the Befana, the old lady who brings presents at Epiphany to all good little Italian children. And that's what these memories are — a present from an old lady.

In 1966 Pat's kitchen still filled with activity until later in the year. Of all the young people around Pat Jordan in the 1960s, none of them to my knowledge turned against him, whatever was to happen in the future. They all spoke of him with affection.

Announcing the opening of the Bookshop

N O T T I N G H A M   S O C I A L I S T
U N I T Y   G R O U P
ooOoo

4 Dame Street
Alfred St. Central
Nottingham

Dear Comrade

You will notice, (from the address) that we have now occupied our new premises;and, of course, we are now more than ever in need of your help. We need assistance in decorating, we need gifts of money, equipment and books with which to stock our new bookshop, (which we hope to open before Christmas, if volunteers are sufficiently forthcoming.)

But weare not merely writing about these matters, which we must take in our stride if we are to build the movement which is needed here, WHAT WE DO WANT TO DOX IS TO REMIND YOU OF OUR WEEK-END SCHOOL, WHICH WILL BE HELD NEXT SATURDAY AND SUNDAY, 16th. AND XX 17th. NOVEMBER.

There will be three sessions:

S A T U R D A Y

Afternoon Session, 2.30-5.00p.m.	THE BRITISH LABOUR MOVEMENT AND IT'S FUTURE

S U N D A Y

Morning Session, 10.30-12-30a.m.	THE COLONIAL REVOLUTION SINCE THE WAR
Afternoon Session, 2.30-5.00p.m.	THE INTERNATIONAL WORKING CLASS MOVEMENT

We have been able to get three first rate tutors, including JOHN FAIRHEADX of the Revolutionary Socialist League, and at least one International figure.

The Place? Almost opposite the new premises; the Clubroom of the "BAY HORSE", the first pub on your left(from St Annes Well Rd.) on Alfred St. Central

Each session will be self contained for the benefit of those who cannot attend for the full period of the school. You will, of course, gain more from the school if you have done some preparatory reading. Among other things we reccomend the following, all of which can be supplied by us providing you write right away.

1) The C.P. and the Labour Left......... by JOHN REDMAN
2) The Permanent Revolution............. by LEON TROTSKY
3) Draft Programme of The Comm. International by LEON TROTSKY

If you are interested in this school, or can put up someone xx from out of town, please fill in the attached form.

Yours fraternally

TERRY GALLOGLY (Secretary)

- -

I shall be attebding the following sessions of the school, for which I enclose 2/6d. fee. (Fee covers all or part of school.)

SATURDAY AFTERNOON....... SUNDAY MORNING....... SUNDAY AFTERNOON.......
Please tick where necessary

I can put up ..... guests on saturday night of school.

Signed

Notes

'Trotsky's Other Son' was chosen by Karl Miller of the *London Review of Books* for the Arts Council *New Stories 8*. Many years later it was found in a secondhand bookshop in Australia by Rob Gould (of Ozleft) who recognised Pat Jordan - although the names were changed - and he put it on the web.

'Winter at the Bookshop' was written to commemorate what would have been Pat Jordan's 90th birthday. The other pieces followed after Ross Bradshaw said he would be interested in publishing.

Acknowledgements

I would like to thank Katherine Hadfield for sharing memories and for her friendship over many years, Julian Atkinson for reminiscences and encouragement (although he does refer to it as *Carry On the IMG*) and for preserving Pat Jordan's letters, Romolo Giannone for enthusiastic recollections of St Ann's and the Bookshop and for putting the writing into electronic form, Ross Bradshaw who agreed to publish and has gone out of his way to find photos and information, Pippa Hennessy for careful proofreading and typesetting, and Tony Simpson for providing parts of letters from Ken Coates, Ralph Schoenman and Chris Farley.

For anyone requiring a more detailed and overall view of the IMG, Ernest Tate's *Revolutionary Activism in the 1950s and 60s, vol. 2, Britain 1965–1970* is recommended.

Also published by Five Leaves

Sneinton People by David Ablitt
64 pages, £5, ISBN 9781910170670

Reds, Rebels and Radicals of Leicestershire, Nottinghamshire and Derbyshire by David Bell
120 pages, £7.99, ISBN 9781910170632

Anarchy 38: Nottingham from the Freedom Press
32 pages, £4, ISBN 9781910170182

Personal Copy: A Memoir of the 1960s by Ray Gosling
256 pages, ISBN 9781910170038 (only available as an ebook, price varies)

Viking Nottinghamshire by Rebecca Gregory
76 pages, £8.99, ISBN 9781910170472

Homes and Places: A History of Nottingham's Council Houses (2nd edition) by Chris Matthews
144 pages, £9.99, ISBN 9780993409332

The Shallow Grave: A Memoir of the Spanish Civil War by Walter Gregory
218 pages, £10, ISBN 9781910170717

Welcome to the Cheap Seats: Silver Screen Portrayals of the British Working Class by Andrew Graves
186 pages, £9.99, ISBN 9781910170625

Exploring Nottinghamshire Writers by Rowena Edlin-White
307 pages, £12.99, ISBN 9781910170359

All available (UK P&P free) from www.fiveleaves.co.uk or from Five Leaves Bookshop (www.fiveleavesbookshop.co.uk, 0115 837 3097)

Other books by Sylvia Riley

Rosehill: portraits of a Midlands city (1989)
Switchboard Operators: short fiction of the 1960s (1994)
Wendy and her Year of Wonders (2008)
Those Summers at Moon Farm (2009)